Dougie Poynter

DINOSAURS ROCK!

MIND-BLOWING FACTS, JOKES AND PHENOMENAL FOSSILS

MACMILLAN

Published 2022 by Macmillan Children's Books
an imprint of Pan Macmillan
The Smithson, 6 Briset Street, London EC1M 5NR
EU representative: Macmillan Publishers Ireland Ltd, 1st Floor,
The Liffey Trust Centre, 117-126 Sheriff Street Upper
Dublin 1, D01 YC43
Associated companies throughout the world
www.panmacmillan.com

ISBN 978-1-5290-2273-5

1 3 5 7 9 8 6 4 2

A CIP catalogue record for this book is available from the British Library.

Printed and bound by CPI Group (UK) Ltd, Croydon CR0 4YY
Designed by Janene Spencer
Editorial: Emma Young and Emma S. Young

Picture Credits: Page 66 Shutterstock / 82 Susannah Maidment / 106 Sarah Slaughter /
109, 110 & 111 Friends of Crystal Palace Dinosaurs / 123 Shutterstock / 129 /
140 Clarissa Koos / 166 & 167 Dave Hone / 170 & 173 Steve Brusatte

CONTENTS

INTRODUCUS 9

BRIEF(ISH) HISTORY OF TIME ON EARTH 29

MESOZOIC PARK 49

LET'S MEET SOME DINOS 63

BAD DAY TO BE A DINO 93

FOSSILS AND PALAEONTOLOGY 117

MODERN SCIENCE 155

MEET THE EXPERTS 182

GLOSSARY 186

ABOUT THE AUTHOR 189

ACKNOWLEDGEMENTS 190

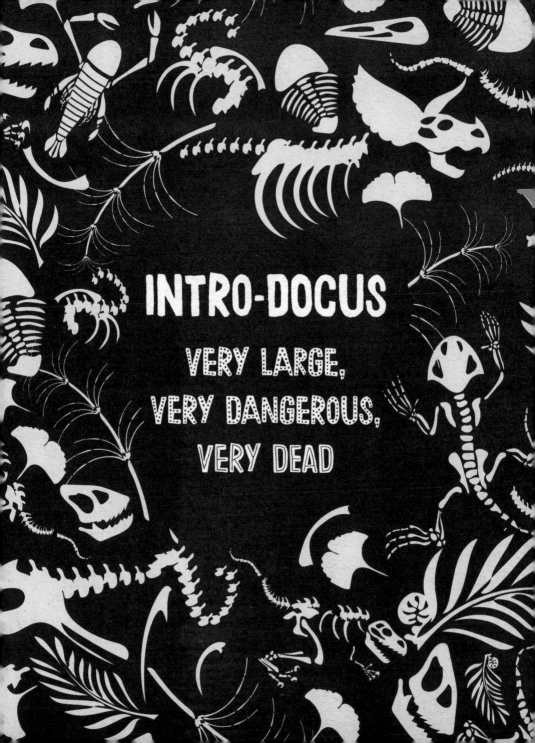

INTRO-DOCUS

VERY LARGE, VERY DANGEROUS, VERY DEAD

PICTURE THIS:

It's a world of giant reptiles. A land of dense forests of green ferns and 6m tall palm trees. The air is thick, sticky, humid and oxygen levels are lower than they are today. All that covers the floor is years' worth of leaf litter and moss and not a single blade of grass (because it hasn't evolved yet) can be seen. Pterosaurs the size of giraffes zoom around the skies like aeroplanes.

IN THE OCEAN marine reptiles like Pliosaur sit at the top of the food chain three times bigger than a great white shark.

AND ON LAND . . .

well it's all kicking off. Herds of Diplodocus as long as blue whales crash through the trees as a Stegosaurus fends off the meat-eating Allosaurus with the giant spikes on its tail. And running around like he owns the place (because he kind of does) is the awesome Tyrannosaurus, with a bite force of thirteen grand pianos slamming down on its prey.

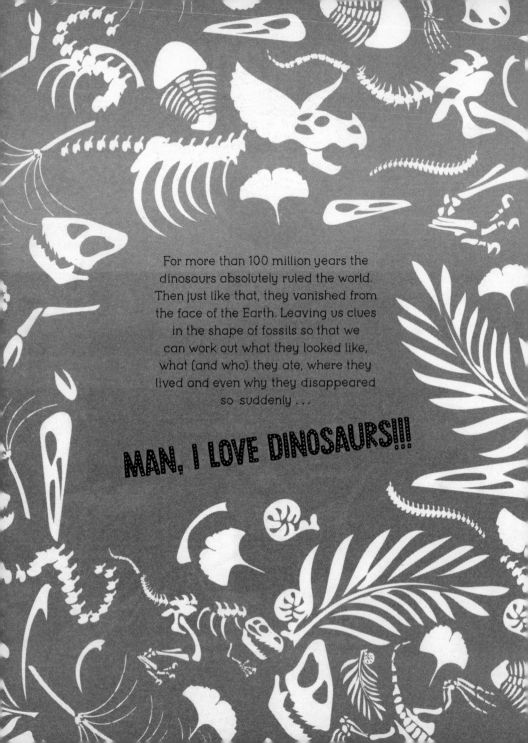

For more than 100 million years the dinosaurs absolutely ruled the world. Then just like that, they vanished from the face of the Earth. Leaving us clues in the shape of fossils so that we can work out what they looked like, what (and who) they ate, where they lived and even why they disappeared so suddenly . . .

MAN, I LOVE DINOSAURS!!!

For as long as I can remember I have been obsessed with dinosaurs. In fact, one of my earliest memories was a cartoon called *Denver The Last Dinosaur* about a dinosaur that lives with a bunch of kids, rides a skateboard and played the guitar (who wouldn't be obsessed?). I didn't quite understand what this awesome dude actually was, so my mum took me to the Natural History Museum to try and explain. Three-year-old me entered the giant gothic building (probably the biggest I had been in at the time) and . . .

MY MIND WAS BLOWN!

Ever since the day when I first laid eyes on those GINORMOUS bones I have been hook, line and sinker in love with these reptiles. I mean, what's not to love? Creatures the size of buses crashing around the Earth with teeth the size of bananas!? SOLD!

I think it's because unlike wizards, unicorns, goblins and dragons, dinosaurs actually existed. I still find that amazing. These giant reptiles ruled our Earth for hundreds of millions of years, they actually walked/stomped around on the very Earth that me and you do and there is actual evidence in fossils to prove it! How awesome is that?

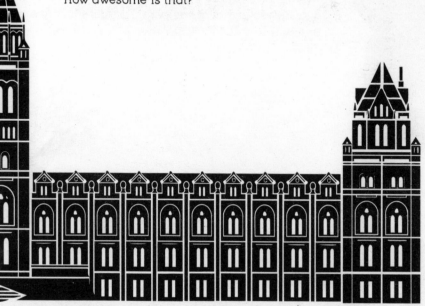

MY FAVOURITE type of dinosaur has always been the **BRACHIOSAURUS**. This dinosaur was a 30-tonne herbivore (meaning it weighed as much as four elephants and only ate vegetation) and was as long as two train carriages. It was basically the largest, friendliest dude on the planet. Walking gracefully around like a huge elephant and chewing on leaves like giant sheep. Oh, and they could live for around one hundred years! Don't get me wrong, I love ALL dinosaurs but I think people's favourite dinosaur says a lot about them. The fact that mine is the Brachiosaurus OBVIOUSLY means I'm cool and calm.

My mate Tom's favourite dinosaur is a T. rex and I think it's because he's BONKERS! Joking. He's a nice dude really. What's yours? And better still, can you spell it?

As I get older (but somehow mentally younger) dinosaurs and natural history remain of huge interest to me. Every day there is a new creature discovered or a little more scientific knowledge uncovered on an animal – like raptors having feathers – which amazes me. It's like the world's largest game of Cluedo. I am not a scientist or a palaeontologist (someone who digs up fossils) or anything else with a smart title, I am simply a huge fan of the world that we live in past and present and I'm so stoked to share what I have learnt with you.

TURN TO PAGE 72 TO READ MORE ABOUT DOUGIE'S FAVOURITE DINOS

HOW BIG WERE
DINOSAUR EGGS?

SINOSAUROPTERYX

MODERN DAY
CHICKEN EGG!

LUFENGOSAURUS

SEGNOSAURUS

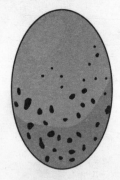

LOURINHANOSAURUS

MASSOSPONDYLUS

CITIPATI

MAIASAURA

DEINONYCHUS

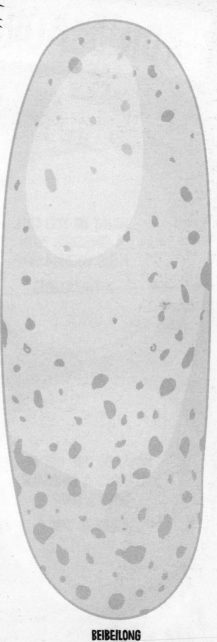

HEYUANNIA

BEIBEILONG

DINOSAUR LOLS

WHAT DO YOU CALL
A DINOSAUR WITH
A BIG VOCABULARY?

A THESAURUS.

KNOCK KNOCK
WHO'S THERE?
IGUANODON
IGUANODON WHO?
IGUANODON'T YOU
REMEMBER ME?

WHAT DO YOU GET IF
YOU CROSS A DINOSAUR
WITH A SHIP?

JURASSIC ARK.

WHAT DO YOU CALL
A PALAEONTOLOGIST WHO
SLEEPS ALL THE TIME?

LAZY BONES.

TRUE OR FALSE?

FLOWERS APPEARED ON EARTH BEFORE THE DINOSAURS.

Turn over to find out

FALSE

EARLY DINOSAURS LIVED IN THE
TRIASSIC PERIOD
(213 MILLION YEARS AGO),
BUT FLOWERING PLANTS
DIDN'T EXIST UNTIL THE
CRETACEOUS PERIOD
(130 MILLION YEARS AGO).

BRIEF(ISH)
HISTORY
OF TIME
ON EARTH

All right, dudes and dudettes, the history of the universe and how our planet came to be the one we know and love today is so HUGE it can be hard to comprehend. But if we shrink that 13.8 BILLION years of history into one calendar year, we can kind of wrap our heads around it. My favourite scientist, Dr Neil deGrasse Tyson, explains it as follows.

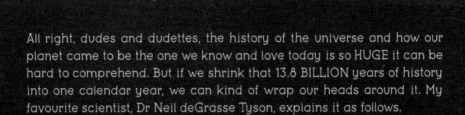

BOOOM CRRRR

On this **COSMIC CALENDAR**, each day is nearly 40 MILLION years, and each month is just over a BILLION years.

31st December at midnight is where we are right now in time. 1st January is the beginning of time as we know it – the Big Bang happens, and the universe and all its contents are thrown out in all directions.

SSSSHHHH!!!

COSMIC

JANUARY	FEBRUARY	MARCH	APRIL	MAY	JUNE
THE BIG BANG. FIRST STARS APPEAR				THIN DISC OF THE MILKY WAY	

THE MONTH OF DECEMBER

1	2	3	4	5	6	7
15 TRACE FOSSILS ONLY		16		17 BONES AND SHELLS		18 VERTEBRATES
22 AMPHIBIANS		23 REPTILES		24 PANGAEA FORMS		25 DINOSAURS
29 TYRANNOSAURIDS		30 DINOSAURS EXTINCT, MAMMALS TAKE OVER ON LAND AND IN SEA.		31 THE FINAL DAY		
				DAWN: APES AND MONKEYS SPLIT	8PM: HUMANS AND CHIMPANZEES SPLIT	

CALENDAR

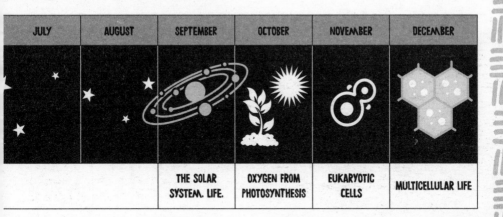

JULY	AUGUST	SEPTEMBER	OCTOBER	NOVEMBER	DECEMBER
		THE SOLAR SYSTEM. LIFE.	OXYGEN FROM PHOTOSYNTHESIS	EUKARYOTIC CELLS	MULTICELLULAR LIFE

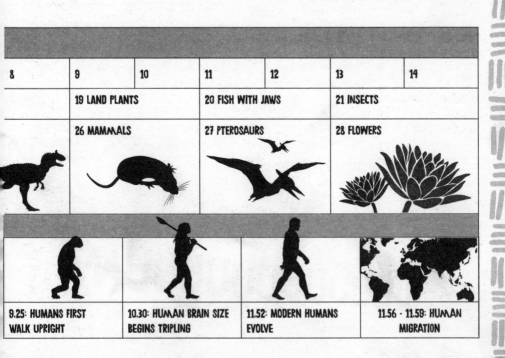

8	9	10	11	12	13	14
	19 LAND PLANTS		20 FISH WITH JAWS		21 INSECTS	
	26 MAMMALS		27 PTEROSAURS		28 FLOWERS	

9.25: HUMANS FIRST WALK UPRIGHT

10.30: HUMAN BRAIN SIZE BEGINS TRIPLING

11.52: MODERN HUMANS EVOLVE

11.56 - 11.59: HUMAN MIGRATION

The crazy part about this is that space itself is included in this . . . so everything was expanding into . . .

NOTHING.

(I'm still getting my brain around that part).

The first stars (suns) form in around February on the Cosmic Calendar. But it's not until September — about 4.6 billion years ago — that Earth even comes into being.

Gas and dust swirling around the Sun lumps together, forming rocks that clump into bigger and bigger balls, a bit like a snowball when you roll it on the ground. One of these balls is Earth.

But it's not freezing, like snow. In fact, it's so hot that the rock is molten. Imagine that! Rock so hot it has actually melted!

While our planet Earth is bubbling away as an endless ocean of lava, another planet called Theia is doing its thing, travelling 20 times faster than a bullet . . . heading right for EARTH!

DUM DUM DUUUUUUUUUUUM!

As the two planets smash into one another (I always imagine this as two melted Maltesers colliding), the debris from the impact creates a ring around Earth. From this ring yet another 'snowball' forms – like a lollipop picking up dirt when it falls out of your mouth and onto the floor. This little guy we will later call The Moon.

For the next few hundred million years, Earth cools and chills out a bit. (It must have been tired.) But asteroids (giant rocks) and comets (dirty snowballs) still smash into our planet, and one or both bring **WATER** (applause!).

At first, it's so hot that this water can only exist as a gas. But by 3.8 billion years ago, Earth's surface has cooled to below 100°C, which as you know, is the boiling point of water. Now, as water vapour escapes from the molten interior out into the cool, it becomes the first rain! Basins in the Earth's **CRUST** fill up with this rain, and the planet is covered in an enormous ocean. The atmosphere still isn't up to much – it was mostly carbon dioxide (what you breathe out) and nitrogen and only a little oxygen. But the really interesting stuff is happening down under the water ...

Volcanic activity below the ocean floor is pumping hot, chemical-rich water up in plumes, out through cracks in the crust. These plumes turn these patches of ocean into an awesome chemical SOUP.

Nobody seems to know how or when but when these chemicals come together, they create one of the most amazing things to ever happen and the most defining part in the making of our planet . . .

The first known life-forms were **BACTERIA**. Though the first fossils – direct evidence of living things – date from 3.5 billion years ago, it's thought that life got going about 300 million years earlier (late September on our Cosmic Calendar). Before long, some learn how to turn sunlight into food. They use photosynthesis just as plants do today – they use the power of sunlight to turn water and carbon dioxide into glucose (sugar, yep bacteria love sugar as much me and you). As these ancient bacteria did this, another magical thing happened. They started to release something so important that none of us can live without it . . . **OXYGEN**.

Oceans, life, some more oxygen . . . it might be sounding a bit more like Earth as we know it. But even a billion years after life began, our planet is still a waterworld, and the atmosphere is definitely still **TOXIC**. Luckily, that is set to change . . .

About 2.4 billion years ago, the mantle (the semi-molten layer just below the Earth's crust) cools enough to support sections of crust that are thick enough to stick up out of the water. (Think about a bowl of soup so thick, a chunk of bread can rest on the top without sinking.) In the geological blink of an eye, Earth suddenly has about two-thirds of the land mass that it has today. And around this time, a group of bacteria called cyanobacteria (which you might know from a pond as blue-green algae) start to churn out huge amounts of oxygen.

Now we have plenty of land, and lots more oxygen, but there's no life on this land yet. And it is shifting . . . The Earth's crust is formed of 'tectonic plates' – giant sections that float on the mantle beneath. (Think of a bowl of thick soup topped with separate chunks of bread. Heavier bits sink down a bit more. These are equivalent to the bits of Earth's crust that are covered with ocean. Lighter sections sit higher in the soup – as land does on Earth . . .) Heat from the mantle underneath makes the plates shuffle around and crash into each other.

Over a billion years and a few different supercontinents later, we now have Rodinia. It looks a little something like this . . .

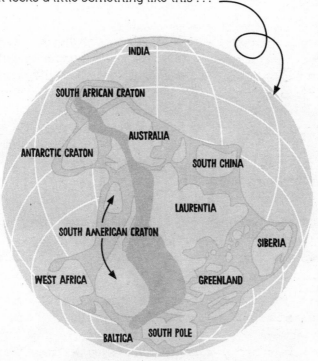

While Rodinia is in play, the first animals – simple sponges – appear in the ocean. But now more shifts in Earth's crust rip Rodinia apart. This, plus an explosion in multicellular algae and sponges, removes so much carbon dioxide from the atmosphere, it's hard for Earth to hold onto its heat . . .

About 715 million years ago, Earth goes through a horrible freezing period. It gets so cold that there is even ice at the equator (the hottest part of the planet). Yes, Earth becomes a giant frozen snowball (this sucks, I hate the cold) in what we believe to be the longest and coldest time the planet has ever known (so, still definitely no sign of any dinosaurs).

It feels like all that hard work to create the perfect conditions for life has been lost and nothing can save it . . . but nothing lasts forever, right? Even bad times!

After millions of years of frozen horribleness, guess who's back to save the day?

The underwater volcanoes melt the ice and begin releasing billions of tonnes of carbon dioxide back into the atmosphere! With the rocks smothered in ice, the carbon dioxide isn't seeping back in. It spreads out like a warm blanket, trapping the Sun's heat in.

Carbon dioxide stabilizes, oxygen rises to be much closer to the level we know and love, and temperatures even out, too. Phew. Life has held on during the cold times, and now we are ready for butt-kicking complex **LIFE-FORMS**.

Starting around 540 million years ago, all kinds of small animals suddenly appear. Mooching around the ocean floor, you can find armoured slug-like creatures called **WIWAXIA**, woodlouse-looking dudes called **TRILOBITES** and the five-eyed **OPABINIA**. This period of massive evolutionary change is called the **CAMBRIAN EXPLOSION**.

OPABINIA

WIWAXIA

TRILOBITES

Animals get bigger and develop skeletons. What seems to be the first creature with a backbone, called **PIKAIA**, appears. A flattened eel-type character about five centimetres long, pikaia is what we believe all back-boned animals, including me and you, evolved from. Weird. Your great- great- great- great- great- great- great- great- great- great-grandparents were shimmying eel-dudes. Hahaha.

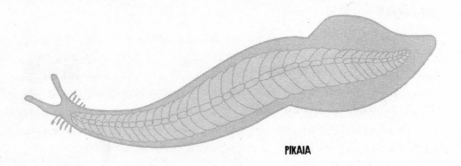

PIKAIA

The ocean is now **BOOMING** with tens of thousands of different life-forms. Planet Earth is on an unstoppable evolutionary roll. We are now at around 18th December on the Cosmic Calendar and, man, have we come a long way.

While the oceans are teeming with amazing life-forms, on land, there's STILL nothing. To be fair, until about 600 million years ago, the Sun's UV radiation was so powerful and deadly that nothing could have lived out of the ocean. By now, though, there's enough oxygen high up in the atmosphere for a gas called ozone to form. Ozone is very good at absorbing the Sun's radiation. It spreads around the planet, acting as a radiation shield.

At last, life on land is possible. But it doesn't exactly jump at the chance. It's about another 160 million years before the oldest known land-dwelling organism appears (in Chad, among other places). A very simple fungus, it doesn't look like much. But it's a start. And at about the same time, algae evolve into water-loving mosses that edge onto land. Fast forward another 55 million years – approaching Christmas on our Cosmic Calendar – and we have a proper half-way step between fish and land animals.

This is **TIKTAALIK**. Technically a fish, it has the usual scales and gills, but also lungs, a head kind of like a crocodile, and four limb-like fins. These fin bones are thick and sturdy, so it can prop itself up in shallow water, and even walk on riverbeds. TIKTAALIK is one of the first creatures to pop its head out of the water and take a look around at a world that no living thing had ever laid eyes upon before. Well done, mate!

Tiktaalik is part fish, part **TETRAPOD** – a word that just means four-limbed. Over time, some tetrapods evolve to make the land, rather than the sea, their home. They become the great ancestors of all things with four limbs, including lizards, birds, mammals and even US. Oh, yes, and on Christmas Day itself – 25th December on our Cosmic Calendar – they give us the gift of . . . **DINOSAURS!**

TIKTAALIK

THE WORLD'S LARGEST DINOSAUR

THE DREAD

NOUGHTUS

26 METRES

DINOSAUR LOLS

WHAT HAS
8 LEGS,
4 EYES
AND 6 HORNS?

A TRICERATOPS
LOOKING IN
THE MIRROR.

WHAT DO YOU CALL
A DINOSAUR WITH
AN EYE PATCH?

DO-YOU-THINK-HE-SAURUS.

WHAT GAME DOES
THE DREADNOUGHTUS
LOVE TO PLAY
WITH HUMANS?

SQUASH.

WHAT DO YOU GET
IF YOU CROSS A DINOSAUR
WITH A TIN OF BEANS?

JURASSIC FART.

TRUE OR FALSE?

DINOSAURS WERE STUPID.

WALNUT

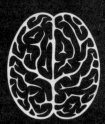

DINOSAUR BRAIN

Turn over to find out

FALSE

KNOWING AS WE DO THAT SOME DINOSAURS HAD TINY BRAINS, AND THAT THEY EVENTUALLY DIED OUT, IT IS EASY TO ASSUME THAT THEY WERE LACKING IN INTELLIGENCE. HOWEVER THERE'S EVIDENCE WHICH SHOWS THAT MANY DINOSAURS WERE PROBABLY MUCH SMARTER THAN WE THINK. LOOKING AFTER THEIR YOUNG AND TRAVELLING IN HERDS FOR PROTECTION, FOR EXAMPLE.

MESOZOIC PARK

One of the most frustrating and confusing things about natural history is how the geologic time scale is divided into periods of such different lengths. It still confuses me now! Particular animals lived in particular times and a lot of the most famous ones never even met. In fact we live closer to when T. rex did than T. rex to a Stegosaurus.

156–144 MILLION YEARS AGO   **68–65.5 MILLION YEARS AGO**   **TODAY**

But if you take a look at the graph on the right it starts to make things a little easier. The further down in the ground you go, the further you travel back in time. By looking at the different layers beneath our feet geologists have been able to uncover what and who lived where and when and even . . . global mass extinctions. These key events of new life and sudden death give us these 'chapters' in Earth's history.

This catalogue (properly called the geologic time scale, or GTS) is organized into 5 different sub groups: eons, eras, periods, epochs and ages. Organizing time up like this allows us to ask questions on different scales. On the larger scale (eons and eras) we can ask: was there life on Earth at this point? If there was, what did it look like? Did it live on water or on land?

Smaller sections of time (periods, epochs, ages) allow us to ask more specific questions like: what was the climate like during this little window of a few million years?

Era	Period/Epoch	Millions of years ago
CENOZOIC	HOLOCENE	10,000 YEARS
	PLEISTOCENE	1.8
	PLIOCENE	5.3
	MIOCENE	23
	OLIGOCENE	33.9
	EOCENE	55.8
	PALEOCENE	65.5
MESOZOIC	CRETACEOUS	145.5
	JURASSIC	199.6
	TRIASSIC	252.2
PALAEOZOIC	PERMIAN	299
	PENNSYLVANIAN	318
	MISSISSIPPIAN	359.2
	DEVONIAN	416
	SILURIAN	443
	ORDOVICIAN	488.3
	CAMBRIAN	542
	PROTEROZOIC	2.5 BILLION
	ARCHEAN	

MILLIONS OF YEARS AGO

EARTH FORMS 4.6 BILLION YEARS AGO

Where I think we should focus is the MESOZOIC era because, well, that's when the dinosaurs lived!

As you can see, within the MESOZOIC era there are three different periods: the Triassic, the Jurassic and the Cretaceous. Each of these periods lasts between 50 and 100 MILLION YEARS (that's a lot of time to get some gnarly evolution in).

The birth of the Mesozoic came from a mass extinction at the end of the Permian period. This extinction wiped out 90% of life on Earth. But a very small group of animals managed to cling on. One group was the ancestors of mammals – like us! From surviving reptiles came the 'archosaurs' – a group of animals that includes the DINOSAURS.

TRIASSIC PERIOD
252.2–199.6 MILLION YEARS AGO

Archosaurs' skulls were lighter than the skulls of their reptile ancestors and most had teeth that were set in deep protective sockets. Plus, they sported a unique respiratory (breathing) system.

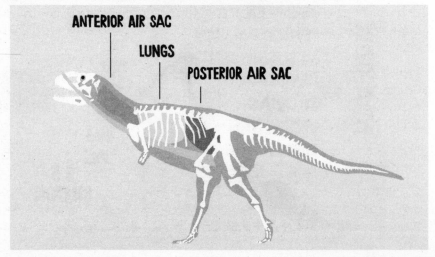

ANTERIOR AIR SAC

LUNGS

POSTERIOR AIR SAC

A selection of air sacs allowed them to breathe more easily and more efficiently in the low-oxygen atmosphere after the Permian extinction – or as some people more grimly call it, The Great Dying. With these awesome adaptations, the archosaurs quickly evolved.

No one knows exactly when the first true dinosaur poked its head out of the ferns, or what it looked like. A good contender is Nyasasaurus, a predator known only from 240-million-year-old fossilized bits of an arm bone and some backbones found in Tanzania, in Africa. But fast forward 10 million years, and the mega-stars – definite dinosaurs – have arrived on the scene.

One of these is Eoraptor. About a metre tall, it was probably an omnivore (it ate meat and plants), and ran around on two legs.

Then there was Herrerasaurus, three times as tall and meaner-looking. This dino was a 'theropod', a group that went on to include T. rex and Velociraptor.

These dinosaurs were members of the same family group, called the Saurischians. They all had the same basic things in common: long necks, long tails and a reptilian body. Now, the most important thing about these animals was a bone in the hips called the pubis, which is one of the three bones that makes up the pelvis (it's the same for me and you . . . yeah we have a pubis). In the Saurischians' case, the pubis bone always pointed down and forward. This is going to be important later, trust me!

Whilst all this commotion was happening down here on land, other groups of archosaurs had different ideas. By the late Triassic, the pterosaurs had become the first backboned animals to take to the skies!

In the ocean, a group of reptiles began to dominate the seas. They include the dolphin-looking Ichthyosaurus, and the long-necked Plesiosaurus.

At this point, there was one big supercontinent called Pangaea. But 201 million years ago, Pangaea began to break apart. What is now North America drifted away from the rest of the supercontinent. A spike in volcanic activity released lots of carbon dioxide, which caused global warming and made the oceans more acidic. Three quarters of the species of animals and plants living in the oceans and on land were wiped out. But this mass extinction wasn't all bad news . . . Almost all the dinosaurs' archosaur competitors died out, and this gave the dinosaurs a free rein to rule their space. Much larger dinosaurs would now rise up out of the volcanic ashes!

JURASSIC PERIOD
199.6–145.5 MILLION YEARS AGO

We are now in the most famous period of the Mesozoic era . . . When the age of the dinosaurs really hits its peak . . . The Jurassic period! It was made famous by one of the greatest movies ever to be made – Jurassic Park. (If you haven't seen this film then we cannot be mates.)

Now, as well as the theropods, we have sauropods, like Diplodocus, who appeared on the scene about 161 million years ago. These dinosaurs had very long necks, long tails, and small heads, and they were herbivores (they ate plants). But they had to compete for food against another rising group of plant-eaters . . .

As well as the 'lizard-hipped' Saurischians, we now have their 'sister group', the Ornithischians. (Though the Ornithischians first appeared in the late Triassic, it's in the Jurassic that they really start to mix things up and diversify.) Remember that pubis bone I was on about earlier? Instead of pointing down and forward, in Ornithischians, the pubis bone pointed backwards. This gave them 'bird-like hips' and much more room for guts! They also had a beak-like mouth and sharp teeth, which meant they could eat some of the toughest plants around. These vegetarians became the eating machines of the Mesozoic era. They became so successful that people recognize many of them today! There were Triceratops, Stegosaurus, Hadrosaurus (a duck-billed dinosaur) and also Pachycephalosaurus (the dude with the dome head that could bash into stuff).

During the Jurassic, dinosaurs also evolved a new line in fashion: **FEATHERS**. Some of these feathery dinosaurs had small bodies and big brains – like **VELOCIRAPTOR**. But there's also a group that are definitely **BIRDS**. This includes the famous **ARCHAEOPTERYX**, which now shares the skies with the pterosaurs.

This really was the golden age of dinosaurs, with the most recognizable characters swanning around doing their thing, eating plants and each other. But their party was about to be shut down yet again . . .

During the Jurassic, what had been Pangaea kept on breaking up. The northern half broke into North America and Eurasia. A chunk that included what's now Antarctica, Madagascar, India and Australia broke off from Africa and South America. New oceans flooded in, and the climate also changed from being hot and dry to warm and damp.

At the end of the Jurassic, there was a series of mini extinctions. Though it's not clear exactly what caused them, it could have been to do with climate cycling and volcanic explosions (again) in the Pacific Ocean. These events shut down all the fun everyone was having in the Jurassic, and invited in our third and final act in the Mesozoic era.

CRETACEOUS PERIOD
145–65.5 MILLION YEARS AGO

The Cretaceous is the longest period of the Mesozoic era. It saw some of the most extreme changes in both animals and plants ever recorded. And things started to get a little more colourful and a little louder! One of its first breakthroughs was the appearance of flowers (yeah, flowers hadn't been around until now!). They first show up in the fossil records about 130 million years ago. (Before this conifers, ferns and cycads were the dominant species of plants.)

Meanwhile, dinosaurs were going through their own revolution. Feathered theropods called coelurosaurs, which hadn't grown much larger than your average dog in the Jurassic, reached new heights in the Cretaceous.

By 125 million years ago, big predatory dinosaurs like **UTAHRAPTOR** (a feathered raptor-looking dude) was hunting in North America and **YUTYRANNUS** (a cousin of T. rex) was terrorizing China.

In the middle of the Cretaceous, a new group of sauropods (those long-necked four-legged dinos) called Titanosaurus were outgrowing all of their Jurassic relatives. Some, like Argentinosaurus are thought to have grown to about 30 metres and weighed 70 metric tons!

In the skies, pterosaurs had grown **WAAAAAAY BIGGER**. By the late Cretaceous, they'd become the largest animals ever to fly in the history of Earth. The giant azhdarchids were as long as giraffes and had a wing-span the size of a small aeroplane. They were more than capable of swooping to eat small dinosaurs.

During the Cretaceous, land masses continued to drift apart.

This led to dinosaur groups becoming more and more isolated and therefore more diverse and more distinct. For example, a group of theropods called tyrannosaurs became the number one predators on land. An early cousin of the tyrannosaurs first appears in the fossil records in the late Jurassic.

By the late Cretaceous, they have developed awesome crunching jaws and swift legs for chasing down their prey. Many dinosaur groups have given rise to their largest and most bizarre members. This was evolution at its finest, showing just how successful these reptiles had become. But all this celebrating was about to come to a very sad end . . .

DINOSAUR LOLS

WHY DID ANKYLOSAURS ENJOY PLAYING GOLF?

THEY ALREADY HAD THEIR OWN CLUBS!

KNOCK KNOCK

WHO'S THERE?

T-REX

T-REX WHO?

T-REX-CELLENT TO SEE YOU!

WHAT DO YOU CALL A DINOSAUR WHO IS GOOD AT MAGIC?

DIPLO-HOCUS-POCUS-DOCUS.

WHY DIDN'T THE DINOSAURS FLY?

IT WAS WAY OVER THEIR HEADS.

TRUE OR FALSE?

DINOSAURS WERE COLD-BLOODED.

Turn over to find out

INCONCLUSIVE

SCIENTISTS HAVE DIFFERING OPINIONS ON THIS — THE LATEST EVIDENCE SUGGESTS THAT ALL THE MAJOR GROUPS OF DINOSAURS WERE WARM-BLOODED BUT IT IS HARD TO FIND CONCLUSIVE EVIDENCE THOUGH SO THIS REMAINS A CHALLENGE FOR FUTURE SCIENTISTS TO UNPICK.

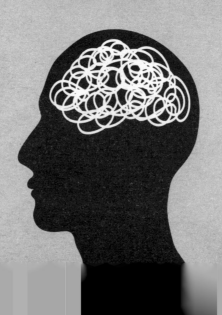

LET'S MEET
SOME DINOS

SAUROPODS

BRACHIOSAURUS

APATOSAURUS

DIPLODOCUS

DREADNOUGHTUS

KEY FEATURES:

Long neck; long tail; tiny heads; walked on all fours. They were the largest of all dinosaurs and perhaps the largest land animals that ever lived.

FAVOURITE FOOD:

Plants. Research suggests they swallowed stones to help break down the plant matter in their stomachs.

Their long necks enabled them to reach the leaves of the tallest trees, similar to the giraffe.

WHEN WERE THEY AROUND?

They first evolved 201—174 million years ago in the Early Jurassic Epoch then became much bigger and highly diverse in the Late Jurassic Epoch (165—145 million years ago). They were still around in the Cretaceous Period (145—65.5 million years ago).

Where were they found? Fossilized sauropod remains have been found on every continent, even Antarctica.

BEST KNOWN SAUROPODS:

Brachiosaurus, Diplodocus, Apatosaurus and the recently disovered Dreadnoughtus.

THAT'S A WHOPPER!

Recently a Dreadnoughtus fossil was found which when alive, palaeontologists believe to weigh around 65 tonnes and was 26 metres long . . . the size of eight or nine T. rex put together!!!

THEROPODS

T-REX

VELOCIRAPTOR

KEY FEATURES:

Stood on two legs, the most feared!

FAVOURITE FOOD:

Smaller herbivores or sick and dying dinosaurs. Yep, these guys were carnivores ...

WHEN WERE THEY AROUND?

From the Middle Triassic Epoch to the Late Cretaceous Epoch (so from 245–65.5 million years ago).

WHERE WERE THEY FOUND?

Theropod remains have been recovered from all continents except Antarctica.

BEST KNOWN THEROPODS:

T. rex, Velociraptor

Most closely related dino to modern day birds.

MEET SUE!

The most famous T. rex to be discovered was one named 'Sue'. Around 90 per cent of her fossil skeleton was found (which is super rare). She was 4m tall and weighed around 8 tonnes. Triceratops, the three-horned plant-eater was among T. rex's prey. This is known because crushed Triceratops frill bone was found in fossilized T. rex poop!

ORNITHOPODS

IGUANODON

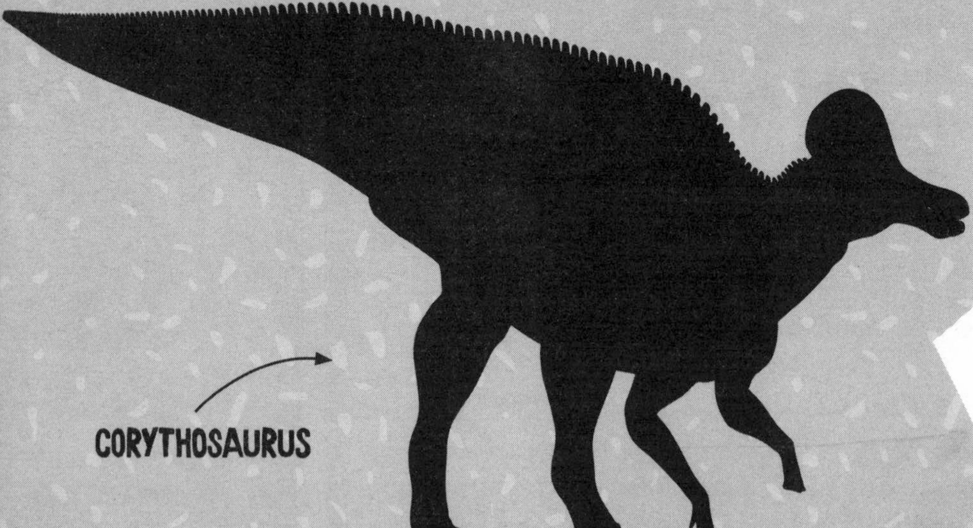

CORYTHOSAURUS

KEY FEATURES:

Bipedal — they could stand on two legs to reach leaves on trees but walked on all fours, with the front legs being more arm-like.

They were one of the most successful and enduring dinosaur groups.

FAVOURITE FOOD:

Plants — some grazed on all four legs as well as eating from trees.

WHEN WERE THEY AROUND?

From the Late Triassic Period to the Late Cretaceous Period (about 229–65.5 million years ago).

WHERE WERE THEY FOUND?

In all seven continents, though they are rarely found in the southern hemisphere.

BEST KNOWN ORNITHOPODS:

Iguanodon — the largest species which reached a length of nine metres — and duck-billed hadrosaur.

FUN FACT:

We know these guys moved in grazing herds because actual fossil footprints of a moving herd have been found! MENTAL!!!

MARGINOCEPHALIA

(MOUTHFUL, RIGHT? IT MEANS 'FRINGED HEADS'.)

STEGOSAURUS

TRICERATOPS

KEY FEATURES:

Armoured plated, horned, tiny brains

FAVOURITE FOOD:

Plants (grazing herbivores — which means eating off the ground or low bushes).

WHEN WERE THEY AROUND?

They first evolved in the Jurassic period and became more common in the Cretaceous.

WHERE WERE THEY FOUND?

Asia and North America.

BEST KNOWN THEROPODS:

Stegosaurus, Triceratops.

FUN FACT/ WHO YOU CALLING STUPID?:

The stegosaur had a brain about the size of a walnut which is the equivalent to us having a seed for a brain. This low functioning brain didn't stop the stegosaur from being successful for tens of millions of years though . . . if you're gonna be dumb you gotta be tough, right? They had some of the most dangerous 'weapons' ever evolved by a plant-eating animal.

DOUGIE'S TOP 5 DINOS!

SO AS YOU CAN PROBABLY TELL BY NOW, I LOVE ALL THE DINOS. BUT HERE ARE THE FIVE THAT BLOW MY MIND THE MOST . . .

1. BRACHIOSAURUS

Ok, so as I said in the Intro-docus, the Brachiosaurus is my favourite dinosaur ever. I've been obsessed with how this giant dude towered over some of the most feared carnivores since I was a kid!

HISTORY: Brachiosaurus was discovered in 1903 in a huge canyon known as 'The Colorado River' by a dude named Elmer S. Riggs.

WHEN? Lived 156–145 million years ago during the late Jurassic period

WEIGHT: Scientists estimate between 25 to 35 tons! This is around the same size as our very own GREY WHALE or as heavy as a heavy-duty excavator.

HEIGHT: Stood a whopping 8.8m tall

LENGTH: 30m long

WHAT DID IT EAT? The Brachiosaurus is one of the most famous vegans that has ever lived. Brachiosaurus had a long neck that allowed it to eat from the highest trees where other dinosaurs couldn't reach up to 9m from the ground. To support its mahoosive body, the gentle giant had to consume 225 kg of food per day, which is what humans consume in three months!

APPEARANCE: Thanks to its disproportionately long neck and longer front legs, this dinosaur stands apart from other sauropod dinosaurs, like Diplodocus and Apatosaurus, which is how it got its name which means 'arm lizard'.

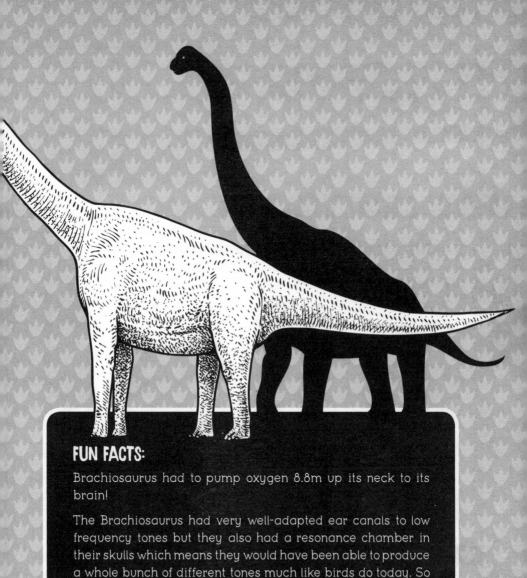

FUN FACTS:

Brachiosaurus had to pump oxygen 8.8m up its neck to its brain!

The Brachiosaurus had very well-adapted ear canals to low frequency tones but they also had a resonance chamber in their skulls which means they would have been able to produce a whole bunch of different tones much like birds do today. So Jurassic Park actually got that right about the singing!

Brachiosaurus had a femur (thigh bone) that was roughly 2m long which is the average height for basketball players.

2. TRICERATOPS

This has got to be one of the most recognizable and radical-looking dinosaurs that ever lived! There's no way you could ever forget this dude with its three horns and head-plate (which I think looks like a backwards cap!). This super powerful plant-eater has got to be one of the most awesome creatures to ever walk this planet. There's something about evolution creating a plant-eating animal with such a gnarly defence mechanism that still blows my mind today. Well done Triceratops, you have made it into my top 5!

HISTORY: The first Triceratops fossil was found in 1887 by George Lyman Cannon.

WHEN? 67—65 million years ago during the Cretaceous period

WEIGHT: Scientists estimate around 5,500 kg!

HEIGHT: This dino grew up to 2.7m tall

LENGTH: 9m long (so it was around the same size as an African elephant)

WHAT DID IT EAT? This gentle giant was a herbivore which means it only ate plants much like our rhinos and elephants. Some of the plants that it ate are still around today, one of which is the fern plant which you can find in most places in the UK.

APPEARANCE: Triceratops had one small horn on its nose and two larger horns above its eye sockets. The larger ones twisted and grew as the dinosaur got older.

FUN FACTS:

The giant skull of the Triceratops made up one third of its body and the largest one found was around 2.4m long!

Scientists are unsure what the purpose was for the frill around its head. It could have provided protection for their neck or been a way that they could recognize another Triceratops.

There are a few Triceratops fossils that actually have teeth marks of a T. rex in the frill – it's pretty cool to think of these two giants going head to head in an epic battle!

3. TYRANNOSAURUS REX

This awesome dude is without doubt the most famous and feared dinosaur by us humans! Tyrannosaurus rex means 'King of the Tyrant Lizards'.

HISTORY: Barnum Brown discovered the first partial T. rex skeleton in 1902 in the USA.

WHEN: 68—65.5 million years ago, during the Cretaceous period

WEIGHT: Scientists estimate around 7,000 kg!

HEIGHT: 3.6m tall

LENGTH: 12m long

WHAT DID IT EAT? This carnivore hunted other dinosaurs but scientists also think that it would have scavenged as well (eating something that another dino had killed).

APPEARANCE:
The T. rex had 60 sharp serrated teeth (each about 15 centimetres long!), a muscular body (including two strong legs) and sharp 10cm long claws.

FUN FACTS:

This dino dude had an insanely powerful bite! A team of scientists examined the T. rex skull and determined that it had a bite force of 8—12,000 pounds per square inch making it the most powerful bite to ever exist on land (its bite was strong enough to crush a car!).

T. rex had a very strong sense of smell and used it to find prey and mates.

Its large tail balanced out its heavy skull (otherwise it might have tipped over!).

4. VELOCIRAPTOR

Raptors are up there with the T. rex as one of the most feared dinosaurs of all time. Jurassic Park turned these guys into infamous villains on a global scale overnight in the early 90s but they may have taken a teeny-weeny bit more artistic licence with the raptors than the other dinos. Beware: some of you may be extremely disappointed.

HISTORY: The first fossils of this species were found in a desert In Mongolia in 1923 by Peter Kaisen.

WHEN: 75 —71 million years ago, during the late Cretaceous period

WEIGHT: Scientists estimate around 7 kg

HEIGHT: About 1m tall (not as tall as they show in Jurassic Park)

LENGTH: 1.8m long (including their tail)

WHAT DID IT EAT?
This speedy carnivore (meat-eater) used its sharp claws to pierce its prey.

APPEARANCE: This dino was about the size of a turkey. It had sharp serrated teeth and retractable claw measuring 8.9cm on each foot! Very recent fossil evidence has shown that raptors were actually covered in feathers!

FUN FACTS:

Velociraptor could run an estimated 24 miles an hour (a bit faster than a human sprinter, not as fast as a motorbike!).

The velociraptor gets its name from two Latin words which mean QUICK and THIEF.

Scientists think that raptors hunted prey much smaller than themselves but were also scavengers (they waited for another dino to make a kill and then swooped in for the scraps).

5. STEGOSAURUS

Did you know that we live closer to when the T. rex lived than the T. rex lived to Stegosaurus? Crazy right? The Stegosaurus lived so long ago it's hard to think that animals like T. rex and raptors hadn't even evolved yet. Around 100 million years separate the two dinosaurs!

HISTORY: The first Stegosaurus fossils were discovered in 1877 by Othniel Charles Marsh in the USA.

WHEN: 155–145 million years ago, during the late Jurassic period

WEIGHT: Scientists estimate around 4,500 kg!

HEIGHT: 4.2m tall

LENGTH: 9m long (about the length of a bus!)

WHAT DID IT EAT? This dinosaur was a very strict herbivore and ate ferns, moss and fruit BUT scientists have also found that occasionally it fell off the veggie wagon and ate a few ROCKS! YUP! ROCKS! Scientists say it swallowed rocks to help it churn up the huge amount of vegetation.

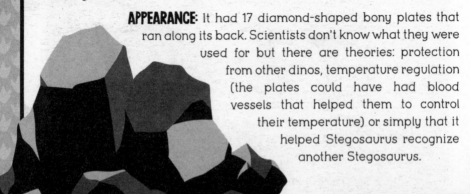

APPEARANCE: It had 17 diamond-shaped bony plates that ran along its back. Scientists don't know what they were used for but there are theories: protection from other dinos, temperature regulation (the plates could have had blood vessels that helped them to control their temperature) or simply that it helped Stegosaurus recognize another Stegosaurus.

FUN FACTS:

Stegosaurus had four large spikes at the end of its tail. Each of those were around 1m long, which it most likely used for defence. Stegosaurus fossils show that their tails had a lot of damage, which could have come from fighting.

The Stegosaurus had a small flat head and a beak very similar to a sea turtle's but get this: even though it was the size of a bus Stegosaurus had a VERY small brain in comparison to its body. It was about the size of a plum!

Originally, scientists thought that the plates were flat along its back (like tiles), but when scientists discovered a partial skeleton that had been held in place by mud, they realized that the plates ran vertically along the spine.

MEET... SUSANNAH MAIDMENT

WHAT'S YOUR NAME AND WHAT DO YOU DO?

My name is Susie and I am a palaeontologist, a fossil researcher of dinosaurs.

WHAT FIRST SPARKED YOUR INTEREST IN PALAEONTOLOGY?

When I was six my grandpa asked me what I wanted to be when I grew up. Back then, I knew I wanted to be either a princess or a scientist.

My grandpa was a scientist so he was quite keen to push me away from my aspirations of being a princess. He asked me what kind of scientist I wanted to be. I actually didn't realize there were different types of scientists, I thought they were all the same thing. I had this image of someone in a white coat pouring chemicals into beakers! So he told me I should be a dinosaur scientist. I was six and I really liked dinosaurs, so I just said OK . . . and that's what I did!

HOW DID YOU END UP WORKING AS A 'RESEARCHER OF DINOSAURS'?

Lots of hard work. To be a palaeontologist you have to have a degree, usually in something like biology or geology – my degree was in geology. Then I did a PhD, which meant I had to spend another four years at university, and then after that I had a number of jobs where I studied fossils and dinosaurs at various universities around the UK, and then eventually I got the amazing job that I have here, which is a 'Researcher of Dinosaurs' at the Natural History Museum.

CAN YOU EXPLAIN TO US WHAT GEOLOGY IS AND HOW IT RELATES TO DINOSAURS?

Geology is the study of rocks. If we can understand how rocks are formed, then we can figure out the type of environments that existed in the past, which in turn helps us to learn about dinosaurs. Studying the layers in a rock can tell you what the environment and plant life around them was like, and in order to learn about dinosaurs we need to look at the sorts of environments that they lived in, their climates and also when specifically in the past they existed. We can't tell that from looking at dinosaur bones, we can only tell that from the rocks.

WHAT HAS BEEN THE HIGHLIGHT OF YOUR CAREER SO FAR?

There are so many really cool things that I get to do. I get to spend tons of time with incredible collections of specimens and I get to do field work. My highlight so far has probably been doing field work in Morocco, where I was lucky enough to name a dinosaur – a new type of stegosaur called Adratiklit, which is the oldest stegosaur in the whole world. The name Adratiklit means 'mountain lizard' in Berber, which is the local language in the Atlas Mountains where the bones were found. Usually dinosaurs are named after Latin or Greek words, but I wanted to call it something in the local language. It's actually really hard to come up with a name, and once you do, you have to check that there's no other animal with the same name – if there is then you have to come up with a different one!

WHAT IS YOUR FAVOURITE DINOSAUR AND WHY?

Probably Stegosaurus ... but I don't really know why! I had a Stegosaurus money box and an inflatable Stegosaurus when I was a kid, and I did my PhD on Stegosaurus. I've worked on them a lot throughout my career, and here at the Natural History Museum, we have the most complete Stegosaurus in the world.

IS IT TRUE THAT THEY WEREN'T VERY SMART AND THAT THEIR BRAINS WERE THE SAME SIZE AS A SAUSAGE?

Well, to be honest their brains were slightly smaller than sausages, probably more satsuma-sized. But brain size isn't necessarily a measure of how intelligent something is. I don't think they were super smart, but I like to think that they weren't as stupid as some people have suggested. For a while, it was actually widely thought that a Stegosaurus brain was in its butt, but that was unfair on them. That being said, they did have the smallest brain per unit of body mass, so the smallest brain for its size, of any dinosaur.

SO WHAT DO YOU THINK ITS DAILY ROUTINE WAS LIKE?

We don't actually know much about the behaviour of Stegosaurus, which is a bit weird as they're such a well-known, iconic dinosaur. The truth is that we don't have that many fossils from them so there are still many unknowns. For example, we don't know whether they lived in herds or separately and we don't know whether they brought up their young or whether they just left them to fend for themselves. There are still so many questions about their behaviour.

DO WE KNOW WHAT THEIR PLATES WERE FOR?

I think they were probably for display, although we're not sure and it's really difficult to test scientifically. If you look at lots of different types of stegosaur – we all know Stegosaurus but actually there are loads of different types of stegosaur from around the world – they all have slightly different shaped plates. I suspect that the plates may have related to them being able to recognize members of their own species. The plates weren't actually attached to the spine, they were just embedded in the skin – quite similar to a crocodile, but bigger.

WHO'S YOUR FAVOURITE PALAEONTOLOGIST?

My favourite palaeontologist is my boss Professor Paul Barrett. He's been a great mentor for me and a massive influence on my career. He does really cool, interesting work and he's named loads of dinosaurs, including the earliest dinosaur that's known, from the Triassic about 243 million years ago, Nyasasaurus, and he's also worked a lot on how dinosaurs feed.

THAT'S SO INTERESTING! HOW DO YOU MEAN?

The first dinosaurs were probably **CARNIVOROUS** (i.e. meat-eaters) or omnivores (meaning they ate both plants and meat), but dinosaurs became herbivores, or plant-eaters, as they evolved. Most reptiles don't chew in their mouths but instead they swallow their food whole. Dinosaurs actually did chew their food (like humans do), and they evolved this ability to chew the food in their mouths. From looking at their teeth we can see what their diet might have been like.

DO YOU HAVE ANY LITTLE KNOWN DINOSAUR FACTS?

My favourite dinosaur fact is that Stegosaurus was already a fossil by the time T. rex lived. Dinosaurs lived on earth for 170 million years, which is a super long time and far too long for us to even be able to imagine. People tend to think that all the dinosaurs were living together, that T. rex and Stegosaurus and Triceratops were all hanging out, but they weren't. They all lived at different times.

WHICH DINOSAUR WOULD HAVE BEEN THE STEGOSAURS' ENEMY?

Probably **ALLOSAURUS**. Allosaurus is found in the same rocks as Stegosaurus in the western US. It was a big meat-eating dinosaur with a big head.

WHAT WOULD YOU MOST LIKE TO FIND OUT ABOUT DINOSAURS THAT ISN'T YET KNOW?

There are so many questions about dinosaurs that I'd love to have answered! Possibly the one I'm most desperate to know is what colours dinosaurs were?

We have some idea about what colour dinosaurs with feathers were – some of the meat-eating dinosaurs we now know were covered in feathers, and we can tell what colour they were by cells that are in the feathers. The shape of the cell is actually related to the colour of the feather. But this doesn't work for all colours, it only works for reds, blacks, browns and whites. Unfortunately for scaly dinosaurs we don't have this information, as the shape of the cell doesn't relate to the colour.

SO WHAT COLOUR WERE THE FEATHERED DINOSAURS?

They've found some that had red stripes and some that were black and white, but we don't know whether there were blues, greens and yellows as those cells are formed in different ways in the feather. There's a dinosaur called Anchiornis that had black and white feathers with red at the ends.

We know that today's herbivores are often camouflaged, for example stripy zebras and spotty giraffes, so it's reasonable to think that some of the dinosaurs could have been camouflaged too.

IF YOU COULD GO BACK IN TIME, WHICH PERIOD WOULD YOU GO TO AND WHAT WOULD YOU DO ONCE YOU GOT THERE?

I'd go the Upper Jurassic period, and I'd probably just hang out and watch. I wouldn't bring any dinosaurs back to the present, because we know that ends badly! I'd look at their behaviour and try and answer some questions about what dinosaurs did. There are lots of questions about dinosaurs in the Upper Jurassic – this was the time when the hugest dinosaurs, the biggest land animals ever to have lived, were on the earth. Dinosaurs like Diplodocus and Apatosaurus were around, and I would love to see how they all lived together and know how there were so many of them all living together in the same place. How they behaved, how they nested, how and whether they brought up their young.

DO YOU HAVE ANY TIPS FOR PEOPLE WHO WOULD LIKE TO GET INTO PALAEONTOLOGY?

Loads of people want to work on dinosaurs, so work really hard at school and if you can focus on science. If you have a local museum go down there and see whether you can help out behind the scenes, do some volunteering to get some experience. And remember that you need to learn about things like geology, maths, biology, ecology and engineering – a whole range of diverse sciences goes into helping us understand how dinosaurs lived.

DINOSAUR LOLS

WHAT DO YOU CALL A
DINOSAUR IN HIGH HEELS?

MY FEET-ARE-SAURUS.

WHY WAS
THE TEENAGE
DINOSAUR SO
GRUMPY?

BECAUSE OF HIS
ROARMONES.

KNOCK KNOCK

WHO'S THERE?

TRICERATOPS

TRICERATOPS WHO?

TRICERATOP OF THE
MORNING TO YOU!

WHAT HAPPENS
WHEN A T-REX
CRASHES ITS CAR?

A TYRANNOSAURUS
WRECK.

TRUE OR FALSE?

SOME DINOSAURS HAD ARMS THAT WERE LONGER THAN A WHOLE ADULT HUMAN.

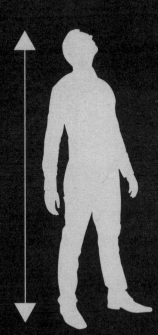

Turn over to find out

TRUE

DEINOCHEIRUS ('HORRIBLE HAND') WAS THE LONGEST-ARMED DINOSAUR. EACH ARM WAS 2.4 METRES LONG AND ENDED IN A THREE-FINGERED HAND WITH LARGE, CURVED CLAWS. SCIENTISTS THINK IT USED THESE CLAWS TO HOOK LEAFY BRANCHES DOWN TOWARDS ITS MOUTH.

BAD DAY
TO BE
A DINO

Sixty-six million years ago, more major shifting in the Earth's crust caused (yet again) more gnarly volcanoes. Just one massive volcano buried much of what is now India in a layer of lava rock more than THREE KILOMETRES deep, and poured vast amounts of poisonous gases into the atmosphere. All these gases likely had a dramatic effect on the climate and oceans. But as if all this volcanic mayhem wasn't enough, something even bigger was on the horizon . . . literally.

Before we get to what that was, first let's leap to a much more recent time: 1980. At this point, scientists know that SOMETHING wiped out all non-bird dinosaurs 65.5 million years ago. That much is obvious – no matter where they look in the world, they can't find any dino fossils that are any younger than this. They think volcanoes and climate change must explain this CATACLYSMIC loss. But then the brilliant American physicist Luis Walter Alvarez and his geologist son, Walter Alvarez (who was also pretty brilliant), came up with a radical theory . . .

Remember how you can dig down into different layers of Earth to work out what happened when? The dad-and-son team focused on a thin layer of clay from the time the dinos vanished. They noticed that it contained an unusual amount of one particular chemical element: a metal called iridium. This stood out, because iridium is incredibly rare. At least, it is in Earth rock . . . But it's common in something else –

ASTEROIDS!

The pair came up with the idea that maybe a massive asteroid impact had killed off the dinosaurs. But if this were true, it would have left a seriously monstrous crater. So where was it?

After a long hunt, scientists narrowed in one spot, in the Gulf of Mexico. There was certainly a dipped zone in the sea bed, and it looked like part of a crater, but they couldn't be sure. In 2016, a team drilled down into it and brought back samples of rock. They found that some of the rock had definitely been MELTED and even torn up from an original position 10km underground.

Here was evidence that this WAS an impact crater and it had been made by something truly HUGE. By studying samples from the crater and other locations, the scientists re-created what must have happened.

SO NOW, WE ZIP BACK TO 65.5 MILLION YEARS AGO . . .

The creatures of the Cretaceous are happily getting on with their lives. Triceratops and T. rex are fighting on land. Pterosaurs are squabbling in the skies. In the ocean, massive-jawed mosasaurs are doing battle with sharks. They have no clue that one of the most momentous events in Earth's entire history is about to happen.

A GIANT ASTEROID, ABOUT 12KM WIDE AND TRAVELLING AT 18 KILOMETRES PER SECOND, IS HEADING STRAIGHT FOR EARTH . . .

BAM!

- IT SMASHES INTO SHALLOW WATER NEAR WHAT'S NOW THE MEXICAN PORT TOWN OF CHICXULUB.

- IT DIGS A HOLE IN EARTH'S CRUST THAT MEASURES 100 KM ACROSS AND 30 KM DEEP.

- THE BOWL-SHAPED HOLE COLLAPSES, CREATING A CRATER THAT IS 200 KM ACROSS AND A FEW KILOMETRES DEEP.

- AT THE SAME TIME, THE CENTRE OF THE IMPACT REBOUNDS, AND ROCK IS LIFTED HIGHER THAN MOUNT EVEREST, BEFORE FALLING BACK.

The impact melts and vaporizes vast amounts of rock. Billions of tonnes of debris and dust are shot up into the atmosphere. Trees ignite and forest fires start to rage. Tsunamis (giant waves) travelling at the speed of a jet plane slam across the oceans. The heat from the strike itself can be felt 1,450 KILOMETRES away.

BUT THE IMPACTS REACH MUCH, MUCH FURTHER THAN THAT . . .

A SHOCKWAVE equivalent to a Magnitude 10 or 11 earthquake ripples around Earth. But even this isn't the worst of it. All the dust and gases thrown up into the atmosphere dim the Sun's light. And this causes global cooling. Scientists think average air temperatures drop below freezing and stay that way for YEARS. The dimming of the Sun's rays also means that many plants in the oceans and on land don't have enough light to photosynthesize. At least HALF of Earth's plant life goes extinct.

Without these plants around, the animals that normally eat them starve. Enormous plant-munchers are among the first to be hit. Massive dinos like the elephant-sized Triceratops had to eat huge amounts of vegetation every day to keep themselves going. Now, they simply can't find enough to survive. With a lack of other dinos to eat, the carnivores, like T. rex begin to die out, too.

Until recently, there was one snag for this story of what happened to wipe out the dinosaurs: there were no dino fossils from the time just before the impact. Some scientists said that perhaps volcanoes and climate change were the number one culprit, after all, and the asteroid came AFTER they'd already gone – kinda like a ninja kick in the direction of someone who's already left the building.

But then a dig in Montana, in the US, turned up the fossilized horn of a Triceratops that, in geological time, died right before the impact. This provided evidence that large dinosaurs were still happily roaming around right up until that fateful moment.

In 2019, scientists also reported another incredible find – a site in North Dakota, in the US, 3,000km from the impact crater, that reveals the fall out of that day. The team found fossils of fish and trees that had been covered in fragments of glassy rock that fell back from the sky. Some fish fossils even had these little rock beads in their gills. They'd literally breathed in the debris. This find helped to confirm just how momentous the impact had been.

As dinos vanished from the land, in the sea, a similar mass-extinction was happening. The large predators, like the plesiosaurs and the mosasaurs, began to disappear from the face of the Earth. In the air, the pterosaurs went too. They'd been an incredible reptile success story: the first creature with a backbone to develop powered flight, some the size of a paper aeroplane but others as big as an F-16 fighter jet — but they met their end.

In total, over three-quarters of all the species on Earth were lost in this Cretaceous-Paleogene extinction (it's given this name as it divides these two periods of time). But ONE group of dinosaurs did make it through. These were bird-dinos. The birds that you can see flying around your garden are descended from those feathered survivors. Not all of this group survived, though.

SO WHY DID SOME MAKE IT, WHILE OTHERS DIDN'T?

Not too many bird fossils from the first few million years after the asteroid impact have been found. But based on studies of modern birds and earth samples, scientists have put together this picture of what probably happened: the birds that lived in trees before the impact WERE wiped out. The forests went, and they did too. But there were also ground-dwelling birds – closer to modern chickens or turkeys than blackbirds or hawks – and they DID survive. These ground-dwellers went on to diversify, and once the forests had re-grown, birds evolved to live in the trees again.

These birds weren't the only stand-out survivors of this terrible extinction, though. Just as the loss of most archosaurs at the end of the Triassic period allowed for the rise of the dinosaurs, the loss of the dinos laid the ground for **MAMMALS** to take over.

Mammals were small (at least, at that time). With little food around, they were better placed to survive. Also, they had varied diets, meaning they weren't so fussy – something that would have come in very handy in the post-Apocalyptic world of plants and animals dying everywhere.

What there was probably a lot of at the time were insects, feeding on the dead. Small animals that could stomach an insect-heavy diet became the main survivors. Mammals, lizards, turtles and birds could have got by as scavengers, dining on the carcasses of dead dinosaurs, fungi, roots and decaying plants, as well as maggots, flies, beetles and cockroaches (what a feast).

Still, even mammals were hit hard by the asteroid strike. Only seven out of every one hundred mammal species that lived right before the impact are found in the fossil record afterwards. But members of all the main mammal groups the placentals, the marsupials and monotremes did make it through the extinction (congrats, guys). And as a group, they bounced back REALLY QUICKLY. Within just 300,000 years (another geological blink of the eye), there were TWICE as many species of mammal hanging out on our planet as there had been before the dinos vanished.

Plant life bounced back, too. Though there were lots of fires after the strike, many flowering plants could weather a burn-off. Before long, the flowers that first bloomed in the Cretaceous period were everywhere! The asteroid survivors might have had to get by on bugs for a while, but at least their world became more colourful.

For the incredible giants of the Mesozoic era though, their impressive size was sadly their biggest downfall. The ones that needed the most food to support their large bodies were the first to go. As our planet entered its next period in time, it was those smaller animals – most probably no bigger than a cat – that inherited the Earth.

AN AVERAGE T-REX WOULD HAVE
NEEDED TO CONSUME 40,000
CALORIES PER DAY.

THAT'S ABOUT 80 HAMBURGERS
OR HALF A GROWN-UP ADULT
OR A WHOLE TEN-YEAR-OLD
CHILD!

80 HAMBURGERS

HALF A GROWN-UP ADULT

A WHOLE TEN-YEAR-OLD CHILD

MEET ...
SARAH SLAUGHTER

DOUGIE: Hi Sarah, how are you doing?

SARAH: Hi Dougie, I'm good thanks. How are you?

DOUGIE: Very well thank you very much. Can you tell us a little bit about what you do?

SARAH: I'm a trustee for the Friends of Crystal Palace Dinosaurs, which is a very small, entirely voluntary run charity. We exist in order to protect and promote the Crystal Palace Dinosaurs. We are a collection of scientists, historians and people who are generally interested in these particular sculptures and what they represent.

DOUGIE: Cool. So, you do this just out of love for history?

SARAH: Correct.

DOUGIE: And this is something you've been interested in since you were a kid?

SARAH: I was born about a mile away from here. My dad is from Penge, so it's just something that's always been in my life.

DOUGIE: Awesome. For the people who don't know, what are the Crystal Palace Dinosaurs?

SARAH: The Crystal Palace Dinosaurs are a collection of sculptures which were built in the 1850s as part of a new destination for Victorians to visit and learn about the world around them. After the Great Exhibition in 1851, Joseph Paxton didn't want his glass 'palace' to be destroyed so he arranged for it to be brought to Sydenham Hill, where a new park was landscaped. The Geological Court, with the sculptures, was a part of that landscape work.

DOUGIE: How many sculptures are there?

SARAH: There is a collection of about thirty sculptures but only four of them are dinosaurs. The rest are amphibious creatures, marine reptiles or mammals that are all extinct.

DOUGIE: How did people react back in the day?

SARAH: The collection of sculptures probably introduced the idea of extinction to the public for the first time and the idea that the world is a lot older than they thought it was and that these creatures once roamed the earth. It must have been quite a surprise! You can imagine that it was something that really shocked people and made them think very deeply about the ideas that they held and the beliefs they held quite strongly.

DOUGIE: It must have been quite controversial at the time?

SARAH: Yes, this was five years before Charles Darwin's book Origin of Species was published in 1859 so you can imagine the reaction would've been quite strong.

DOUGIE: Yeah. Some of the sculptures here are based on one very small fragment of fossil, right?

SARAH: Correct. Not very much had been found at that time so the artist, Benjamin Waterhouse Hawkins, drew on his knowledge of anatomy of current animals but he also worked with eminent scientists of the day, such as Richard Owen, to try and depict the sculptures as accurately as he possibly could. He wanted people to learn from them but also be interested in them from an artistic point of view.

DOUGIE: Nice! Which sculpture is the furthest from what we think the animal looked like?

SARAH: Possibly the Labyrinthodontia – they are the ones that look like big frogs. They would have looked quite different. More like crocodiles than they are depicted in these sculptures.

DOUGIE: I remember those ones! Giant frogs with really horrible teeth! Which sculpture is the most scientifically accurate?

SARAH: Probably the Megoloceros (Irish Elk).

DOUGIE: Which of these sculptures is the most popular with visitors?

SARAH: I can see what people tag us in, and the photos people take of the dinosaurs, and the two Iguanodon sculptures pop up on Instagram the most. 'Meg' the Megaloceros is also very popular and she has her own Twitter account – although I don't run it!

DOUGIE: Well she runs it obviously!

SARAH: I'm not sure her feet would work on a mobile phone!

DOUGIE: Haha. Is the Iguanodon the sculpture where they accidentally put the thumb bone on the nose?

SARAH: Yeah that's right. Looking at modern-day iguanas, some of them do have a spike on their nose so the artists might have looked at that and thought it was found on the nose.

DOUGIE: It does kind of make sense. There is a rhino iguana that has a horn-type thing so it's not a million miles away . . . How do you maintain and look after all of these sculptures? Do you have to get a boat out to the island?

SARAH: Recently, we've been wading using waders that come up to our chest. There was a bridge that the Victorians put in but it had to be removed a few years ago and unfortunately it wasn't replaced. In 2018, the Friends of Crystal Palace Dinosaurs did a crowdfunding exercise to raise money to put in a new bridge.

DOUGIE: That's awesome! What are your plans for Dino Island moving forward?

SARAH: Once we have the new bridge in place, which is currently in progress, we will be able to apply for more funding in order to conserve them properly. They have had some conservation work done through the years but you can see that some are seriously neglected. For example, the antlers on the Megaloceros are coming off. And some of the dinosaurs have some very serious cracks in them. We need to get access to the island so that we can go in and assess what damage has been done, work out what work needs to be done and then maintain it afterwards. At the same time, the charity exists to spread knowledge about the sculptures and educate people about them and their existence.

DOUGIE: What is an average day like for you here?

SARAH: I'm a volunteer with the dinosaurs so for me, day-to-day, I run the social media accounts. In my spare time, I will look through Instagram, Twitter and Facebook to see if people have taken pictures or posted. People can ask us questions and they can get in contact through our website as well. As trustees, we have a responsibility to use funds that we receive and run projects like building the new bridge. We also run Dino Days in September – we have events like tours of the island or book readings!

DOUGIE: The sculptures are amazing! Thank you so much for your time.

DINOSAUR LOLS

WHAT DO YOU CALL
A SINGING GROUP
OF DINOSAURS?

TYRANNO-CHORUS.

WHAT DO YOU
GET IF YOU CROSS
A TRICERATOPS
WITH A RABBIT?

TRICERA-HOPS.

WHAT KIND OF
DINOSAUR LISTENS
TO HIP-HOP?

A RAPTOR.

WHAT DID THE
ANGRY PALAEONTOLOGIST
SAY TO THE OTHER
PALAEONTOLOGIST?

'I'VE GOT A BONE
TO PICK WITH YOU.'

TRUE OR FALSE?

DINOSAURS ARE EXTINCT

Turn over to find out

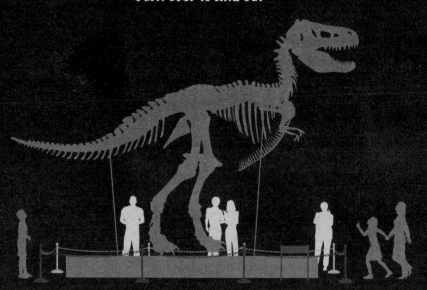

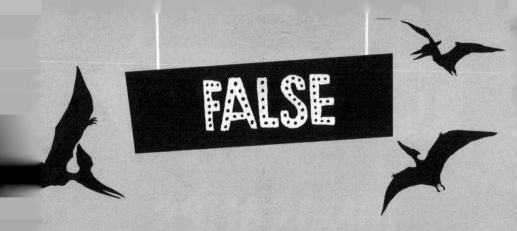

FALSE

SOME DINOSAURS ARE STILL WITH US,
WE KNOW THEM BETTER AS BIRDS. THEY
EVOLVED FROM MEAT-EATING DINOSAURS
AND ARE STILL EVOLVING TODAY.

THAT WILL MAKE YOU LOOK TWICE
AT THAT PIGEON PECKING A HAM
SANDWICH ON THE STREET!

FOSSILS
AND
PALAEONTOLOGY

HOW TO MAKE A FOSSIL
(AND WHERE IN THE WORLD
THEY ARE FOUND)

I am super lucky to own a few fossils myself. I have part of a T. rex's shin bone (only a very small part) and a tiny raptor tooth. I also have a few casts of things like a sabre-toothed tiger tooth and an Iguanodon's thumb nail! One of the coolest ones I have, and it grosses people out, is my coprolite. That is quite simply . . . fossilized dinosaur poop! But what is a fossil? What is the gruesome process an animal's body must go through to be permanently frozen in time?

The first thing to say is that, technically speaking, a fossil is any preserved remains of something that was once alive. You can have fossilized footprints, shells, bones, and trees, as well as, yes, poop. Even coal is a fossil — it's a 'fossil fuel' formed from dead, decayed plants that were pressed together over millions of years.

When a dinosaur died, its body would usually get broken down or taken apart by hungry scavengers, insects and bacteria (gross . . . circle of life, though, innit) or even flowing water. Any soft bits that didn't get eaten would start to rot away. All the juicy stuff like skin, fat, muscles and organs, would disappear, until all you were left with were the hard parts, like bones, teeth and horns. But even these hard bits weren't all fossilized – not by a long way. Whether a fossil got made or not totally depended on where and even how the dino died.

Few dino fossils come from what would have been jungles or mountains. Most are thought to be of animals that were close to water – like a lake, swamp or a river – and they either died right before the region flooded, or they got washed into the water, and were quickly buried.

WHY? Because to be fossilized, a dead animal usually has to be covered with water-containing sediment (generally mud, sand or dirt). And when something actually dies in water, it sinks to the bottom and is quickly covered. This slows down decomposition, and makes fossilization more likely.

MOST DINO FOSSILS WERE MADE IN THIS WAY:

1. The animal dies and starts to rot or be eaten.

2. Its body is covered by sediment.

3. Water seeps into tiny spaces inside the bones and teeth. This water contains minerals, which slowly crystallize in these spaces, hardening the remains. (This takes a LONG time. Even up to millions of years.)

4. At the same time, the sediment above gradually builds up and turns to rock, encasing the fossil.

(When dino poop is fossilized, it's usually the bits of bones and teeth from a carnivore's prey that are preserved through this process.)

Because the mineral make-up of sediment is different all over the world, we end up with a whole range of coloured fossils — from bright orange to chocolate brown to light tan and even green!

The quicker the burying/mineralizing process can start, the better. In fact (as far as fossilization is concerned, anyway!) death by being swamped with something damp is the ultimate way to go.

For example, Big Mama, in the Mongolian Dinosaur Museum, is an amazing **OVIRAPTOR** fossil. Palaeontologists believe the poor dino died when a sand dune collapsed after heavy rains, crushing it (sad face).

OVIRAPTOR actually means **EGG THIEF.** It got this name because the first specimen was found near a nest of eggs that were thought to belong to another species. But many years later, palaeontologists found a fossilized oviraptor embryo in an identical egg. Then the following year, **BIG MAMA** was found with a clutch of these eggs beneath her. Far from being an egg-thieving criminal, she was a cute, caring mother, brooding her babies at the time of her sudden death (another sad face).

MONGOLIA is a great spot to look for dino fossils for two reasons. One: 80 million years ago, it was a dino paradise – lovely and humid, and full of lakes. Two: all the more recent winds and harsh winters have weathered away the top layers of rock, leaving those ancient remains close to the surface.

Generally, the best spots to look for dino fossils today are places like this: regions of Earth that were lush and wet in dino times, but then either surface weathering or shifts in the Earth's crust have have made the fossils accessible.

Now, next time you are at a museum, try this out . . . As we know, fossils are basically rock. And if I remember correctly, rock is pretty heavy. So if you see what looks like a dino skeleton hanging from the ceiling, the chances are that they are not the real fossilized bones, but a cast (like when you break your leg) of the fossil. But if you see any behind a protective glass case or on the ground then they are probably the real thing.

MEET MY FAVOURITE FOSSIL HUNTERS

MARY ANNING:
THERE'S SOMETHING ABOUT MARY

Mary Anning was born in Dorset, in 1799. She lived in Lyme Regis – now known as the Jurassic Coast because of all the fossils found there from Jurassic times.

In Mary's day fossil hunters often thought that they were looking at bones of existing species rather than long-extinct creatures. At the age of twelve, her first big discovery was a whole **ICHTHYOSAURUS SKELETON** which people thought was a crocodile or a monster (the name Ichthyosaurus means 'fish lizard'). In fact, Mary had uncovered an ancient reptile that lived 201–194 million years ago. It still contained the visible remains of prehistoric fish in its stomach – gross!

She also discovered a **PLESIOSAUR** (a long-necked marine reptile) and a **PTEROSAUR** pterosaur – her first winged discovery. These awesome creatures are believed to have been the biggest ever flying animals.

Mary, who had been collecting and selling fossils since the age of five, was an expert in preparation, gently removing rocks from the fossils and cleaning them. The famous tongue-twister 'she sells sea shells on the sea shore' is rumoured to have been written about her. Her work was often dangerous – she survived a landslide aged thirty while out hunting for fossils.

One of my favourite Mary facts is that she solved the mystery of what some of the strange rocks (**COPROLITES**) she and other fossil hunters were finding actually were – fossilized poop!

Because she was a woman, and working class, sadly Mary was not always recognized for her achievements, and many of her incredible discoveries were published by male scientists who didn't even mention her name. Today she is celebrated as one of the most important fossil hunters in history.

OTHNIEL C. MARSH AND EDWARD DRIVER COPE: DINOSAUR WARS

First meeting in 1864, these two American fossil hunters were friends who later fell out and became massive rivals, each determined to be the top palaeontologist in the world! Cope had a fiery temper, whereas Marsh was calmer and more reserved – but as it turned out, they both loved a good argument . . .

Things first went wrong when Cope showed Marsh his **ELASMOSAURUS** fossil – a large marine reptile from the Late Cretaceous period. Marsh noticed that the vertebrae (backbones) were pointing backwards, and asked a third scientist, Joseph Leidy, for his opinion. Leidy picked up the head and placed it on the other end – which Cope had thought was the tail. Realizing his error, Cope rushed around trying to collect the copies of the article he'd written about his discovery, while Marsh set about publicising the embarrassing mistake.

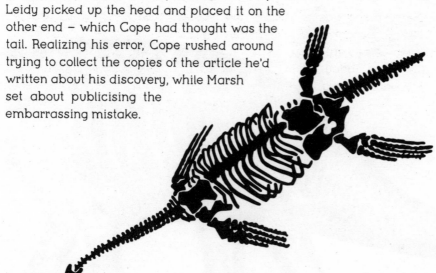

Over the next 15 years, the warring academics went out of their way to outshine and embarrass each other, stealing each other's finds, destroying dinosaur bones, spreading harmful gossip and attacking each other's reputations amongst other scientists. In the meantime they liberally spent money on their own expeditions (mostly in Western America: Colorado, Nebraska and Wyoming) and on purchasing more dinosaur bones for their collections from other fossil hunters.

Sadly Marsh and Cope bankrupted themselves in the process, losing the respect of friends and colleagues along the way. They made frequent scientific errors in their rush to outdo each other. However, they left a valuable scientific legacy behind: their period of fiercely competitive fossil hunting led to over 130 new dinosaur species being discovered between them, such as the now well-known **DIPLODOCUS, TRICERATOPS** and **STEGOSAURUS.**

DINO BLOOPERS 1

One of the things I love most about dinosaurs is that there's always something new being discovered – and it often turns out that something we thought was fact is just a load of baloney! But heeeeeey we all make mistakes, right? Here's a look at some of my personal favourite dinosaur bloopers . . .

DINOSAURS OF CRYSTAL PALACE

Crystal Palace in London is AMAZING for a couple of reasons:

1. It has giant statues of dinosaurs.

2. These statues mark the point when scientists were first beginning to realize that dinosaurs had roamed the earth millions of years ago. These awesome scientists were discovering for the first time that a whole species of giant animals had lived and died out long before humans started running around the world – think how mind boggling and controversial that would have been!

So, it's pretty understandable, given that they had never seen such creatures before, that Richard Owen and Benjamin Waterhouse Hawkins may have imagined the dinosaurs a little . . . weird. Check out the first interpretations of the Iguanodon.

A hundred and a bit years later, after more specimens of the Iguanodon have been found, we now know it's more likely that the animal's structure was quite different. Scientists realized that the horn didn't belong on the end of the nose, as they had first thought, but was actually on their front feet!

THE T.REX'S VISON

In the very unlikely event that you ever come across a T. rex, please do the complete opposite of everything the people in Jurassic Park do. The one I'm getting at being 'Don't move, he can't see you if you don't move . . . Yeah, you might want to ignore that and GET THE HECKLES OUT OF THERE AS FAST AS YOU CAN.

The idea that a T. rex could only detect motion is pretty out there, especially if you compare it to the modern apex predators of today. I mean, imagine if a lion could only see its prey when it was moving? To be an effective predator you need great senses and enough brain power to be able to outsmart your prey.

Scientists now think that the T. rex probably had more binocular range than a hawk and better visual clarity than an eagle. On top of this it probably had a great sense of smell . . . so yeah, MOVE!

PALAEONTOLOGY AND
THE TOOLS OF THE TRADE

One of the most exciting parts of the job for any palaeontologist is finding a new fossil. Imagine ... there you are, strolling over ground that's about 67 million years old, when **WOAH**, a bit of fossilized Triceratops toe catches your eye.

Maybe you're thinking: that sounds really low tech (not to mention extremely lucky). Surely modern dino-hunters have all kinds of equipment to scan the ground, to search for exciting fossils buried beneath their feet?

The answer is: not really ... A few bits of kit have been tried out, but none has turned out to be that helpful. One example is 'ground penetrating radar' (which uses radar pulses to 'look' beneath the surface). This kit is brilliant for turning up something that's really different in density from what's around it – a buried stone wall, say, surrounded by soil and debris. But as we know, dino fossils are basically rock, and radar's not great for distinguishing one type of rock from another.

In any case, the world's top fossil-hunting sites tend to be in remote, inaccessible places, like deserts and 'badlands' (a type of terrain that's been seriously eroded – so where really old rock is at the surface). These spots aren't exactly ideal for big, bulky machines. But they're fine for ...

US!

Experienced researchers know where on the planet they're most likely to find dino fossils. So, mostly, they simply go there,

AND LOOK . . .

AND LOOK . . .

Their eyes, and their knowledge of the shapes of hundreds if not thousands of different dino bones, are their biggest assets.

THE CONTENTS OF THEIR KIT BAG WILL LOOK SOMETHING LIKE THIS:

So what happens if you're an exploring researcher and you **THINK** you've found a bit of dino bone sticking out of some rock, but you're not sure?

First, you might tap it with a knife. If you hear a metallic, chinking noise, that can be the giveaway that it's a fossilized bone, which is a little more fragile and porous than the rock around it.

You might also use the tongue test. Yes ... this means **LICKING** it. If it sticks hard to your tongue, this is a killer clue that you've got a mineral-rich dino fossil on your hands. Well, your mouth. (Warning: try to make sure it's not actually a bit of dried up animal poo first! The two can be confused.)

What you're **REALLY** hoping to discover, of course, is not just a little bit of bone, but an entire skeleton. So your next job is to survey the area, digging **EXTREMELY** carefully, to try to work out exactly what you've found.

Whenever you find a bone, you put a little flag beside it (so no one else in your team accidentally stands on it). Then you mark its exact location on the planet using a Global Positioning System device.

Next, you might pour glue on the exposed bones to harden them. (Especially if these bones are small, they're going to be fragile.)

Then you'll dig out as much rock as you can around the specimen, with a good solid supporting section left underneath.

The next job is to wrap the fossil like the best, most precious Christmas present ever, in a padded 'jacket' of paper and plaster – the kind used for a cast if you break a bone. As it goes into a crate, it gets even more padding. At last, it's ready for transport back to the museum, or the lab.

Now, you need to release your dino skeleton from its rocky prison.

The usual way to do this is to physically get rid of everything that isn't fossil. This happens in stages.

1. Big chunks of rock are removed using a **HAMMER AND CHISEL.**

2. **A PNEUMATIC AIRPEN** – a tool with a tiny vibrating tip – is used to slowly but delicately chip away at rock that's closer to the fossil itself.

3. Something very like a **DENTIST'S DRILL** is used to grind away down to a rock coating just a tenth of a millimetre thick.

4. **NEEDLES** are used to poke away the last particles of rock.

Another method is to use a weak acid to very slowly (I mean slowly; this can take months) and gently remove the rock.

Dino specialists do still use these methods to get at a fossil. But there are also some seriously high-tech new techniques. They can let you look at a fossil without even removing it from its surrounding rock . . .

CT (COMPUTED TOMOGRAPHY)

CT scanners use doses of X-rays that are powerful enough to penetrate rock. This produces thousands of individual images – digital 'slices' – through the specimen. Software then reconstructs these slices into a 3D image. This technique lets palaeontologists view fragile fossils while they're still encased in rock. It also lets them look inside fossils, without breaking them open – to reveal embryos inside fossil eggs, for example.

X-RAYS PLUS ELECTRON BEAMS

This technique can generate incredibly detailed images of a fossil still in its rocky tomb, and of what's inside that fossil. A team in Germany recently used it to identify different species of teeny pollen grains inside the stomach of a 47-million-year-old bird.

SYNCHROTRON X-RAY IMAGING

For this one, you need a particle accelerator (a massive machine that can blast samples with X-rays thousands of times more powerful than those used in a CT scan). This produces INCREDIBLY sharp images, showing up 3D structures just ONE-HUNDREDTH the thickness of a hair on your head.

All this tech is transforming what palaeontologists can do with fossils. It's helping them to work out how long-extinct animals walked, flew or swam. At Stanford University in the US, for example, researchers are using computer programs, fed with digitized T. rex bones, to try to work out if it really could run, and if so, how fast its prey would have had to sprint to escape.

The images can also be fed into 3D printers, to make replicas of the skeletons – or even of what the animal looked like when it was alive.

The synchrotron technique is so powerful, it can identify chemical traces in bits of ancient skin and feathers, and so clues to their colours. It's revealed, for example, that Archaeopteryx had feathers that were light-coloured (perhaps white) with dark edges and tips.

A dude called Jakob Vinther at the University of Bristol has done all kinds of high-tech work on dino colours. He's even used a combination of colour-mapping and 3D reconstruction to create a super-realistic model of a little dark-backed, pale-bellied guy called Psittacosaurus (the name means 'parrot-lizard') who died in China 120 million years ago.

Another technique giving incredible results is a lot simpler. Using UV (ultra-violet) lamps, all kinds of invisible features have literally come to light – pieces of skin and feathers, even bits of muscle. Some museums now regularly use UV light to check over a fossil while they do the rock-stripping, to make sure they're not accidentally getting rid of something really important. Luckily, this was done with a 151-million-year-old fossil of Juravenator starki. UV examination showed that though it had pebbly skin, it was also at least partly covered in 'proto-feathers' – also known as 'dino-fuzz'. Yes, this guy was fluffy!

What this all goes to show is that these days, experts are just as likely to make incredible dino discoveries from the comfort of their lab as by walking a windswept desert. **BOTH** types of exploration are important.

ANKYLOSAURUS AND TRICERATOPS, BOTH LARGE PLANT-EATERS, WERE BOTH 8 METRES LONG, ABOUT THE LENGTH OF A LONDON DOUBLE-DECKER BUS.

← 8 METRES →

ANKYLOSAURUS

TRICERATOPS

TYRANNOSAURUS REX, A LARGE MEAT-EATER, WAS 12.3 METRES LONG, ABOUT THE LENGTH OF ONE-AND-A-HALF LONDON DOUBLE-DECKER BUSES, OR TWO-THIRDS THE LENGTH OF A BOWLING LANE, OR THE LENGTH OF THREE VOLKSWAGEN BEETLES.

12.3 METRES

TYRANNOSAURUS REX

BRONTOSAURUS, A VERY LARGE PLANT-EATER, WAS 22 METRES LONG, ABOUT THE LENGTH OF ONE-AND-A-HALF TRACTOR TRAILERS,

R THE LENGTH OF TWO FALLEN TELEPHONE POLES, OR A LITTLE OVER
HE LENGTH OF A BOWLING LANE.

MEET ...
CLARISSA KOOS
AKA DINOGIRL

WHAT'S YOUR NAME AND WHAT DO YOU DO?

My name is Clarissa Koos, and I am currently studying palaeontology at Montana State University.

HOW DID YOU FIRST BECOME INTERESTED IN DINOSAURS?

My go-to response to this question is always that I loved dinosaurs like any other kid, but I never grew out of it. That probably isn't fully true — I was obsessed with dinosaurs. I had a bookshelf dedicated to dinosaur books, and every morning I would read one of those books. I had a basket full of dinosaur toys that I would constantly play with. I loved going to science museums to see the fossils, and I watched as many dinosaur documentaries as I could. But when I was around 10 years old, I have a specific memory of when my love of dinosaurs really took hold. I was playing the video game 'Fossil Fighters,' and when I was watching the dinosaur Afrovenator standing menacingly in the fog, I realized how amazing and cool dinosaurs are, and my fate to become a palaeontologist was sealed. Since then, I have continued to love dinosaurs, and that love has taken me to where I am today.

TELL US THE STORY OF HOW YOU EARNED THE NICKNAME 'DINOGIRL'.

It started when I went to some dinosaur talks at the Los Angeles Natural History Museum. The final talk was given by palaeontologist Luis Chiappe, and at the end of it, my parents had me introduce myself to him. He then introduced me to the fossil preparator Maureen Walsh, and she let me clean some of the fossils at the museum. Because of Maureen, Luis invited me to their dig site the following summer in Utah when I was eleven. After this dig site, I was introduced to Greg Wilson, and he invited me out to their dig site in eastern Montana. The day before I arrived at the campgrounds, one of the volunteers there, Geoff Harrison, found a new dig site. The day after I arrived, he took me out to the new site. He asked me if he could name the site in my honour because of the passion that I showed. Of course I said yes, so the site became Clarissa. At the time, I had no idea what an amazing thing this was going to be for me. The following summer we were able to excavate the fossil, and it was discovered that it was an Edmontosaurus. The fossils of Clarissa are now in the collections of the Burke Museum in Seattle, Washington. That year Greg Wilson had his Dig Field School out there, which is where I met Denise Porcello. She is a second grade teacher, and she had always wanted to write a children's book. When she met me, she knew she wanted her book to be about me and my experiences in palaeontology. This was where I got the nickname Dinogirl. It was the name of the book, and I became Dinogirl because of it. In summer 2017, I found a dig site of my own. I was out looking for fossils with my friend in eastern Montana, and while out there, I saw some bone trailing up a hillside. I decided to check it out, and at the top I found a rib, some vertebrae, and a horn. I had found a small juvenile Triceratops. It didn't have the best preservation, so it wasn't collected, but it was such an amazing experience to find a fossil.

WHAT'S IT LIKE TO GO ON A DIG? TELL US ABOUT SOME OF THE PLACES YOU'VE BEEN.

It is a lot of hard work and long days. The movies always like to show a perfectly articulated (put together) fossil that only needs a little bit of dirt brushed off. Reality is much more difficult. It's usually very hot with no shade, and the rock is typically very hard. Once the rock was so hard that I got to use a jackhammer to chip away at the rock so that we could make significant process. Lots of times there are rattlesnakes. One dig site I went to involved a several-mile hike just to get to the fossil! Despite all of these challenges, going out to a dig site is really rewarding. You get to meet and get to know so many amazing people, and it's incredible to find the bones of a creature that hasn't been seen on the planet for millions of years. It is also very peaceful and quiet out in the badlands, which can be relaxing in a weird way. A lot of unique challenges like to appear at dig sites, which make for some really good stories to tell friends. For example, over the span of three days, I rode in four different cars that had a flat tyre. Apparently in the two weeks that the University of Washington group had been out there, they had more than 30 flat tyres!

The thing I find amazing is to be standing exactly where a dinosaur stood millions upon millions of years ago. I've worked in two places: The Hell Creek Formation in eastern Montana and in a quarry near Bluff, Utah. I've gone to the Hell Creek Formation seven times, and I've been to Utah twice. So far, the dinosaurs I have worked on in Montana are Triceratops, Edmontosaurus, and Tyrannosaurus, and in Utah, I worked in a large quarry where there was a Camarasaurus. It was hard to tell what other species were there, but they would be dinosaurs from the Jurassic period.

WHAT'S YOUR FAVOURITE DINOSAUR AND WHY?

This one is a tough question. Is saying that my favourite dinosaur is my pet bird lame? Going back to the question, I will always have a soft spot for Stegosaurus and Velociraptor because they were my favourites when I was little, but right now I have to say my favourite is called Anchiornis. It was a small, feathered dinosaur from China that had wings on both its arms and its legs. What makes this little fella really cool is that it was the second dinosaur where palaeontologists were able to figure out its colours. It was mostly dark grey with black-and-white wings and a red fluffy crest on its head. As someone who loves drawing dinosaurs, I find it really exciting that I can draw a dinosaur and it might look very similar to what it actually looked like when it was alive.

WHO'S YOUR FAVOURITE PALAEONTOLOGIST AND WHY?

My favourite palaeontologist has to be Luis Chiappe at the Los Angeles County Natural History Museum. He was the first palaeontologist that my parents had me introduce myself to back when I was 10 years old, and he was the catalyst that put me where I am today. Besides Luis being the one that helped start my palaeontology career, I also find his field of research really interesting. His focus is on early birds, specifically the early birds in the Jehol region of China. The transition from dinosaur to bird is a long and complicated transition to understand, so I have the utmost respect for him and his work.

WHAT'S IT LIKE STUDYING PALAEONTOLOGY AT UNIVERSITY/COLLEGE?

So far it has been an amazing experience! I have met so many other dinosaur lovers since getting to college, and my classes have been really interesting. Right now, I am taking a class on dinosaurs, which has been fun. I haven't done many palaeontology-related classes yet because I am only in my first year, but I have been starting some projects of my own outside of the classroom. College has given me the opportunity to do illustrations for my friend's press release of his senior thesis, and I'll be doing artwork for the museum partnered with our college, Museum of the Rockies. Through my years at college, I will be updating some of the old artwork in the museum, as well as adding some murals depicting the life that lived in Montana 65.5 million years ago. I have a good feeling that a lot of amazing things are in store for me in college and beyond.

WHAT ARE YOUR CAREER DREAMS FOR THE FUTURE?

My current career goal is to become a scientific illustrator. I have always loved to draw animals, both alive and extinct, so becoming a scientific illustrator can combine my love of drawing and my love of science. For those who don't know what a scientific illustrator is, they are the ones that create the drawings in museums, news articles, scientific papers, and some of the dinosaur books for kids. I don't really see myself as a professor or a researcher, but I do see myself going into scientific illustration. Even though I love going to dig sites and helping discover and dig up dinosaurs, I think that the best way I can help the world of palaeontology is through my illustrations.

DO YOU HAVE ANY TIPS FOR BUDDING PALAEONTOLOGISTS?

I have two main suggestions. My first one is that if there is something that you are truly passionate about, pursue it. It is really important for your career to be something that you enjoy, so if you love dinosaurs and palaeontology, don't let anything stop you. My other tip is to understand the importance of communication. Through the years, my mum has told me the importance of talking to people in the field of palaeontology and making connections. The more connections you have, the more people you will meet, and the more likely an amazing opportunity will come up. Being friendly and open to people can have amazing effects that can literally change your life, like it has for me.

THE WORLD'S SMALLEST DINOSAUR

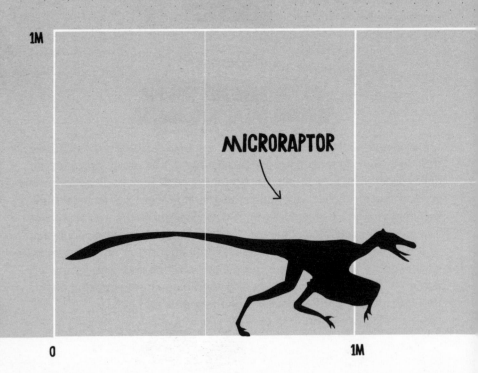

1M

MICRORAPTOR

0   1M

HUMAN

2M

3M

DINO BLOOPERS 2

DILOPHOSAURUS

Dilophosaurus had an awesome supporting role in the first Jurassic Park movie and was arguably one of the coolest dinosaurs in the film. I mean, it didn't even bother to show up in the movie until right near the end! But this crazy, venom spitting, turkey-sounding killer was unfortunately nothing like the real thing.

The dino in the movie was about the size of a Labrador, but in real life these guys would have grown up to 1.8 metres tall – that's quite a lot taller than your average human. It was one of the first large land predators EVER, dating back over 100 million years ago (that's a good 50 million years before old REXY appeared). In the movie, the shape of the dino's head was pretty similar to that of the raptors, but the fossils that have been dug up have a unique and flat pointy shape to it. The super rad neck frill that the dino displayed just before launching itself on to the villain of the movie (Dennis) is unfortunately just made up for effect. Yeah, that bummed me out too.

KANGAROO REX 1905

If you have ever seen a super old stop animation dino movie, or an even an old looking drawing of a T. rex, the chances are the dino kind of looked like a weird, lizard-like kangaroo, standing upright and dragging its tail along the ground. That's because early palaeontologists believed that dinosaurs were actually a mix of kangaroos and lizards. After more complete remains of the same animal were discovered, palaeontologists realized that they had pieced the T. rex together in the wrong way, and by flipping around existing bones they were able to create more realistic and agile-looking rexies.

THE WHOLE FEATHER THING!

Probably the most recent blooper you have heard of is the whole 'Dinosaurs had feathers' thing. The discovery of feathers on well-known theropod dinosaurs, like the T. rex and the raptors, has changed the way we see and reconstruct dinosaurs forever, confirming the link between them and birds. Before this discovery, all of our theropod dinosaurs were NAKED and thought to be covered in thick scales like reptiles. During the 90s a whole lot of feathered dinosaur fossils were discovered, drastically changing all previous reconstructions and bringing us a kind of cuter, fluffier version of our favourite dinosaurs.

Controversially, many theropods are still reconstructed without feathers and this makes palaeontologists maaaaaad! In fact, I recently spoke to a palaeontologist at the Natural History Museum in London about the feathers, and it turns out that certain colours leave a particular trace in the cells, so you can tell what colours the feathers were. How cool is that? We are just that little bit closer to knowing what colour dinosaurs were!

DINOSAUR LOLS

WHAT DOES
A TRICERATOPS
SIT ON?

ITS TRICERA-BOTTOM.

WHY DID THE
ARCHAEOPTERYX
CATCH THE WORM?

BECAUSE IT WAS
AN EARLY BIRD!

WHY DID
THE DINOSAUR
CROSS THE ROAD?

CHICKENS HADN'T
EVOLVED YET.

WHICH SONG DOES
THE T-REX FIND DIFFICULT?

IF YOU'RE HAPPY
AND YOU KNOW IT
CLAP YOUR HANDS.

TRUE OR FALSE?

THE TALLEST DINOSAUR WAS A PLANT-EATER.

TRUE

A BRACHIOSAURUS MIGHT HAVE GROWN TO 12 METRES TALL, ALLOWING IT TO REACH THE LEAVES OF THE TALLEST TREES.

MODERN
SCIENCE

EVERY YEAR?

EVERY MONTH?

IN FACT,
IT'S CLOSER TO ABOUT
ONE EVERY WEEK!

We're in a new golden age of dino discovery! So let's take a look at just a few of the amazing species that have been found recently — either out in the field, or hiding in plain sight in museum cabinets.

Like this guy . . .

Its official Greek name is **THANATOTHERISTES**. Its English translation is a bit more memorable . . .

REAPER OF DEATH!

The craziest bit about this find is that the 79.5-million-year-old skull fragments were actually found in 2010 by a couple strolling along a river in Alberta, Canada. They contacted palaeontologists from a nearby museum, who went out and collected them. But it took almost another DECADE before a local student noticed the bits of bone stashed away in a cabinet, and realized that they looked unfamiliar.

After two years of study, he finally revealed that they belong to a new, 8-metre long 'tyrannosaurid', a group that includes tyrannosaurs like T. rex. No, the Reaper of Death wasn't as towering as a T. rex, but it was a fearsome predator and fighter, and it has the marks to prove it: a scar 10cm long snaking across its right upper jaw.

While the Reaper of Death was huge, some newly-discovered relatives fall at the other end of the scale. Take **MOROS INTREPIDUS**, a 96-million-year-old tyrannosaur that was only about as big as a deer. (The name Moros means the 'embodiment of impending doom' – it might have been a scrappy little dude, but no one would have said that about its later tyrannosaur relatives!)

The same year that Moros was discovered (2019), a feathered dinosaur with bat-type wings was unearthed in China, and a new sauropod with defensive spines that stuck out of its neck was reported from South America. And these were just A FEW of the dozens of new species reported in that one year.

All these new finds are helping palaeontologists to make broader discoveries about how different dinosaurs evolved, and how they lived.

As we know, the name dinosaur means 'terrible lizard'. We humans are warm-blooded (like other mammals, and also birds). We use tiny food-burning factories inside our cells to generate heat, to keep our body temperature stable. Cold-blooded reptiles, like lizards and crocodiles, don't bother with this, using the Sun to warm them instead. When it's nice and sunny, they move about and do their thing. When it's cold, they cool down, which means they slow down, too.

For a long time, it was thought that dinos were cold-blooded, too.

But then most palaeontologists came to agree that the feathered theropods that gave rise to birds were actually warm-blooded. Then people started asking:

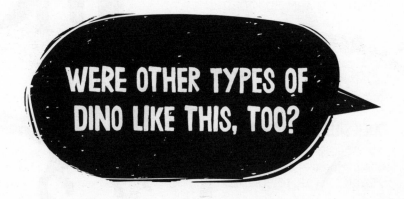

WERE OTHER TYPES OF DINO LIKE THIS, TOO?

Recently, scientists developed a brilliant technique for analyzing dino eggshells, to work out the body temperature of the mother when the shell was formed. And, in 2020, this technique revealed some killer results:

TROODON FORMOSUS
(a theropod):
body temperature: up to 38°C.
VERDICT: WARM-BLOODED

DWARF TITANOSAUR
(a sauropod):
body temperature: 36°C
VERDICT: WARM-BLOODED

DUCK-BILLED DINOSAUR
(an ornithischian)
body temperature: 44°C
VERDICT: WARM-BLOODED

These species represent the three different major groups of dinosaur. It's unlikely that warm-bloodedness evolved independently in all of them. So, while there's still some debate, this suggests that all dinos fell into this category, and a common ancestor was warm-blooded, too.

If it is likely that dinos were all warm-blooded, this helps with some other big outstanding questions about them, too. Like:

HOW FAST – AND HOW FAR – COULD THEY RUN?

Mammals and birds have a much bigger 'aerobic capacity' than cold-blooded lizards. An animal's aerobic capacity is a measure of how good its heart and lungs are at getting oxygen to its muscles. The more oxygen you can get to your muscles, the longer you can run (or fly). Also, muscles work better when they're warm. A warm-blooded creature can leap into action faster than a cold-blooded one. All this suggests that dinos were highly active, with plenty of stamina for finding food, or fighting.

But despite all the amazing dino finds in recent years, there are still ALL KINDS of questions that palaeontologists don't know the answer to. Like:

WHICH WAS THE BIGGEST DINOSAUR?

Odds are it was a **TITANIC SAUROPOD**, and a few contenders for the title have been put forwards. These include **DIPLODOCUS** and also **SUPERSAURUS** (a 35-tonne GIANT, which it kinda had to be, to earn a name like that), as well as Argentinosaurus. But we don't have complete skeletons for all these species. So it's hard to know just how big they were. The biggest ever dino could still be out there, waiting to be found . . .

DID DINOS REALLY HUNT IN PACKS (AS THE RAPTORS DO IN JURASSIC PARK?)

When the film came out, this was controversial. But since then, we've got more clues that at least some raptors did gang up like wolves to chase down prey. Some of the best recent evidence comes from a block of sandstone excavated in Utah, in the US. It contains the fossilized remains of at least six **UTAHRAPTORS** plus a **HERBIVORE**, which it's thought they were chasing (right into a patch of quicksand . . . Unlucky for them, but kinda lucky for us . . .). But whether raptors DEFINITELY went hunting together is still debated.

No one really knows. But by looking very closely at fossilized bone, we can work out whether it came from a young or an old dino. For some species, like **T. REX**, it's even possible to estimate how old it was when it died. The next step is to compare a range of dino bones with bones from modern animals whose exact age is known. This could give us more clues as to how long they lived for.

The thing is, one of the biggest stumbling blocks to learning more about dinos and how they lived is actually this: a lack of detailed knowledge about animals that are alive today!

EXAMPLE . . . You can learn a lot about the size and shape
of dino brains by closely examining their skulls. (CT scanning has been REALLY helpful for this.) And if we know the exact shape of a dino's brain, we can work out the size of at least some individual regions. When a US team did this, they thought, GREAT – now we can compare our reconstructed dino brain with a map of how all these regions are important for behaviour in a living bird, to give us clues to DINO behaviour.

PROBLEM: That map didn't exist. So they had to make it for
themselves, using little scanning helmets that they put on birds!

(It's early days, but the work suggests that bird relatives like **TYRANNOSAURS** and **VELOCIRAPTORS** WERE brainy.)

Anyway, if you're feeling like we now know **SO MUCH** about dinos, by the time I grow up there'll be nothing left to discover . . .

NO WAY!
THERE ARE PLENTY OF BIG QUESTIONS THAT WILL KEEP FUTURE PALAEONTOLOGISTS BUSY FOR MANY, **MANY** YEARS TO COME.

MEET...
DAVE HONE

WHAT'S YOUR NAME AND WHAT DO YOU DO?

I'm Dave Hone and I'm a palaeontologist, which means I study extinct organisms. In my case, I specialize in dinosaurs and some of their relatives and I also write and talk about them so other people can learn too.

DO YOU JUST COVER DINOSAUR STORIES?

I mostly cover dinosaurs as that is what I am most interested in and they are also very popular for people to read about. But I also write about other fossil reptiles like pterosaurs and ichthyosaurs or other fossils from the time of the dinosaurs including the insects, plants and mammals. Occasionally I get asked to cover things that are much older or more recent, like mammoths, and I sometimes write about living animals too.

WHAT'S IT LIKE GOING ON A DIG?

I've been on digs in China, Mexico and Canada — all rather similar as there are lots of rocks and sometimes lots of bones! It's not always as exciting as people think. You spend a lot of time out getting hot and tired and not finding very much. Happily, it's nice to be out with your friends and the scenery is often very beautiful. And of course, when you do make an important or interesting find it's really amazing, although then you spend your time getting hot and tired digging a big hole to get it out of the ground.

My best ever find was of most of a skeleton of an early tyrannosaur called **GUANLONG** that I discovered in China, it was only the third ever specimen of this animal.

Every day is different and amazing things can happen. Once while digging, I stopped and took a break in the shade and fell asleep. When I woke up, I noticed I was surrounded by eggshells – I'd passed out in a dinosaur nest and not even noticed!

WHAT'S YOUR FAVOURITE DINOSAUR AND WHY?

The sauropod **AMARGASAURUS** from Argentina. I like it because it's really weird and everything a sauropod usually isn't. Most of them are really big with long necks and they don't go in for any of the flashy horns and spikes and display features that other dinosaurs do. However, **AMARGASAURUS** is small (well, small for a sauropod, it's still elephant-sized), with a neck so short it could barely reach the ground, but it had two sets of huge and cool spines running down its neck.

WHO'S YOUR FAVOURITE PALAEONTOLOGIST AND WHY?

I'm really not sure I have a favourite, though Franz Nopcsa is hard not to admire given his incredibly interesting life and he made some very cool dinosaur discoveries in Eastern Europe.

FAVOURITE STORY YOU'VE COVERED?

It's always nice to be able to write about your own research and discoveries and I've been lucky enough to be able to do that quite a few times. Probably the best was doing **REGALICERATOPS**, a really interesting dinosaur from Canada. The work was done by some friends of mine so I know the fossil and the research well and it was nice to be able to talk about my friends and their work.

REGALICERATOPS is a ceratopsian and a close relative of **TRICERATOPS**. However, unlike its famous cousin it has 'reversed' its horns and has two little horns over the eye and a big one on the nose. It also has unusually large spikes at the edge of its frill making it unique.

CAN YOU EXPLODE A MYTH OR MISCONCEPTION ABOUT DINOSAURS?

The biggest one is that all extinct animals, or all extinct reptiles are dinosaurs. The pterosaurs and plesiosaurs, as well as sabre-toothed tigers, ammonites and all kinds of other things are not dinosaurs. Birds however, are the direct descendants of dinosaurs and so birds are dinosaurs, they are still alive!

ANY TIPS FOR HOW BUDDING PALAEONTOLOGISTS CAN GET INVOLVED?

Remember than fossils are just one part of palaeontology. To really understand ancient life, you need to know about all kinds of bits of science – physics, maths, chemistry and geology as well as biology. Just learning about dinosaurs will only get you so far.

MEET...
STEVE BRUSATTE

WHAT'S YOUR NAME AND WHAT DO YOU DO?

Steve Brusatte: palaeontologist and professor at the University of Edinburgh, Scotland.

WHAT FIRST SPARKED YOUR INTEREST IN DINOSAURS?

I had no interest in dinosaurs when I was a young child. In fact, science was my least favourite class in school. But then everything changed when I was 14 years old. My youngest brother Chris loved dinosaurs, and he asked me to help him with a school project, and quickly I became fascinated with dinosaurs too!

HOW DID YOU END UP GETTING YOUR JOB?

I kept hopping back and forth across the Atlantic Ocean, until somebody gave me my dream job. I grew up in the USA and went to university in Chicago. Then I moved to England to do a Master's degree. Then I moved back to the USA, with my new English wife, to do my PhD in New York. And then we moved back to the United Kingdom when the University of Edinburgh in Scotland offered me a job. It was a whirlwind few years!

WHAT IS YOUR CAREER HIGHLIGHT SO FAR?

In 2018 I wrote a book about dinosaurs called *The Rise and Fall of the Dinosaurs*. Bill Clinton, the former American president, read the book and said it was his favourite book of the year. I couldn't believe it!

WHAT'S YOUR FAVOURITE DINOSAUR AND WHY?

Tyrannosaurus rex. I know that many people love T. rex. It might seem like a boring choice. But to me, T. rex is one of the most amazing animals that has ever evolved. It was the largest pure meat-eater that ever lived on land in the entire history of the Earth. It was the size of a bus and bit so hard that it crushed the bones of its prey. I think T. rex is more fantastic than any dragon or monster that humans have created in fiction or movies – and T. rex was real!

WHO'S YOUR FAVOURITE PALAEONTOLOGIST AND WHY?

Mary Anning. She lived in the early 1800s on the south coast of England. She grew up poor and never had the chance for an education. But she had an excellent eye for fossils. She made her first big discovery when she was only 12 years old! For the rest of her life she collected skeletons, which she sold to the wealthy gentlemen scientists of the day. She never got the proper credit she deserved, but today she is recognized as one of the greatest fossil hunters of all time!

CAN YOU SHARE AN AMAZING BUT LITTLE-KNOWN DINOSAUR FACT?

T. rex is closer in time to us than it was to Brontosaurus! Crazy huh? T. rex lived 65.5 million years ago, which means it is separated from humans by 65.5 million years. Brontosaurus lived 150 million years ago, which means it was separated from T. rex by 84 million years. When T. rex was alive, every Brontosaurus fossil that ever formed was already in the ground.

HOW IS NEW TECHNOLOGY CHANGING PALAEONTOLOGY?

Technology doesn't help us find fossils. We still use the same techniques as fossil hunters in the 1800s: we walk around and look to see what is poking out of the rock. But, once we find a fossil, new technologies help us study that fossil, to understand what it was like as a real living, breathing, moving, growing animal. Palaeontologists often use technologies borrowed from other fields, like engineering and chemistry.

HOW HAS TECHNOLOGY SUCH AS SCANNERS CHANGED PALAEONTOLOGY? WHAT TYPE OF THINGS DO YOU USE? HOW MUCH DIFFERENCE DOES IT MAKE TO WHAT YOU CAN LEARN?

Like many palaeontologists, I use **CT SCANNERS** to study dinosaur fossils. Medical doctors use CT scanners – which are basically high-powered X-ray machines – to see inside our bodies, to find out if we might have an injury. Palaeontologists use scanners to see inside of dinosaur fossils.

For example, I often CT scan dinosaur heads, to see how big their brains were, which helps us understand how smart dinosaurs were.

WHAT ARE THE BEST THINGS YOU HAVE DISCOVERED?

My favourite discovery is one that I made with my friend and fellow palaeontologist Tom Challands, on the Isle of Skye in Scotland, in 2015. We were walking back to our cars after a long day of searching for fossils. We didn't have much luck. Until we spotted these giant holes in the rock, each one the size of a car tyre. There were over 100 of them. And they formed a pattern – a left-right, left-right zigzag sequence. We then noticed that these holes had impressions of toes and claws. They were dinosaur tracks! These particular handprints and footprints were made by a 170-million-year-old long-necked dinosaur that weighed as much as three elephants put together!

YOU HAVE BEEN MAKING SOME AMAZING DISCOVERIES ON THE ISLE OF SKYE IN SCOTLAND. CAN YOU TELL US WHAT YOU HAVE FOUND AND WHAT IT MEANS?

We have also found many other fossils on the Isle of Skye. We have found the footprints of meat-eating dinosaurs the size of jeeps, stegosaurs with plates on their backs, and duck-billed dinosaurs that chewed leaves with their beaks. We've also found bones of dinosaurs, plus the crocodiles and **PTEROSAURS** (pterodactyls) that lived with them. Together these fossils reveal a real Jurassic Park! About 170 million years ago, in the middle of the Jurassic period, Scotland was full of dinosaurs. It was much warmer and more humid then, and many of these dinosaurs lived on beaches and even would have walked or swum in the shallow water. Some of these dinosaurs, like the long-necked ones that left the handprints and footprints, were some of the first truly giant dinosaurs to ever live. Their descendants would later become larger than jet aeroplanes!

WHAT WOULD YOU MOST LIKE TO KNOW ABOUT THE DINOSAURS THAT WE DON'T HAVE AN ANSWER FOR YET?

About 200 million years ago, at the end of the Triassic Period, the supercontinent of Pangaea (the giant land-mass that the first dinosaurs lived on) began to split apart. This is why there are many individual continents today, like North America and Europe. When Pangaea split, big volcanoes erupted, for abut 600,000 years! Those volcanoes caused the temperature to rise very quickly, which led to a mass extinction, in which thousands of species all over the world died. The giant crocodiles and salamanders that were the competitors of early dinosaurs, and the dominant animals on Pangaea, were among the victims. But, for some reason, dinosaurs survived. And we don't know why! This is a mystery for a smart young palaeontologist to solve.

DO YOU HAVE ANY TIPS FOR ANYONE WHO MIGHT LIKE TO DO A JOB LIKE YOURS ONE DAY?

The most important quality of a scientist is curiosity. Always keep exploring, always keep asking questions about the world around you, always keep reading and learning new things. In school, take as many science classes as you can, but don't forget about English class too – all good scientists need to be able to communicate. Use the internet to follow the latest dinosaur discoveries. And when you are old enough, start to collect your own fossils! Get a guidebook from the library or use the internet to see what rocks are located close to where you live, and then go out to explore. See if you can find your own fossils. There is no greater feeling than discovering a fossil that is tens of millions of years old, a clue from a vanished world. And you are the first person to ever see it!

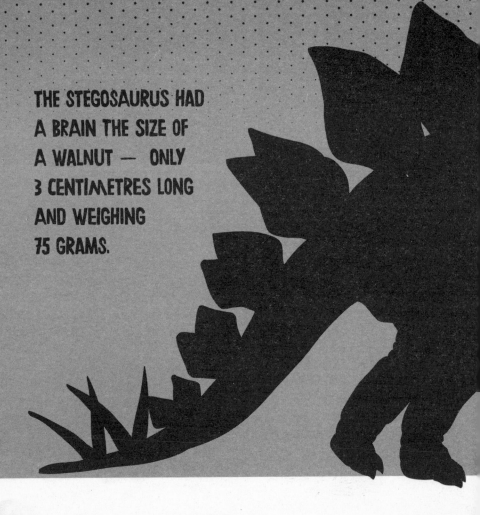

TINIEST-BRAINED DINO

THE STEGOSAURUS HAD
A BRAIN THE SIZE OF
A WALNUT — ONLY
3 CENTIMETRES LONG
AND WEIGHING
75 GRAMS.

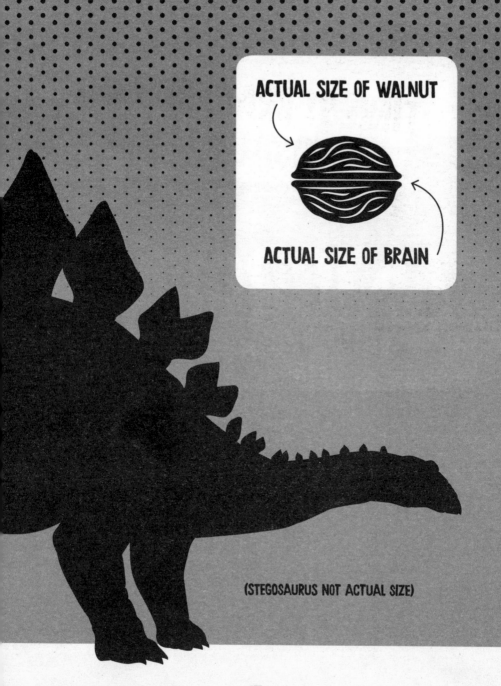

ACTUAL SIZE OF WALNUT

ACTUAL SIZE OF BRAIN

(STEGOSAURUS NOT ACTUAL SIZE)

MICROPACHY

PRONOUNCED MY-CRO-PACK-EE-SEFF-AH-LOW-SORE-US

Despite its long name the Micropachycephalosaurus was a tiny dinosaur that probably weighed as much as a domestic cat.

CEPHALOSAURUS

MESOZOIC ERA

MEET THE EXPERTS

Sarah Slaughter

Sarah Slaughter is a PhD History student, and in her spare time volunteers as a trustee with Friends of Crystal Palace Dinosaurs. Sarah runs the charity's social media (cpdinosaurs), conducts history tours for members of the public, and works with schools to share information about the site.

Steve Brusatte

Steve Brusatte is the author of the bestselling The Rise and Fall of the Dinosaurs and its junior edition The Age of the Dinosaurs, for young dinosaur-enthusiasts. He is a paleontologist on the faculty of the School of GeoSciences at the University of Edinburgh in Scotland. He grew up in the Midwestern United States and has a BS in Geophysical Sciences from the University of Chicago, MSc in Palaeobiology from the University of Bristol (UK), and PhD in Earth and Environmental Sciences from Columbia University in New York. Steve is widely recognized as one of the leading paleontologists of his generation. He has written over one hundred peer-reviewed scientific papers during his decade of research in the field, named and described over ten new species of dinosaurs, and led groundbreaking studies on how dinosaurs rose to dominance and went extinct. One of his particular research interests is the evolutionary transition between dinosaurs and birds and he is a noted specialist on the anatomy, genealogy, and evolution of the carnivorous dinosaurs like Tyrannosaurus and Velociraptor.

Susannah Maidment

Susannah Maidment is a dinosaur researcher and curator of fossil archosaurs at the Natural History Museum, London. Her research focuses on the bird-hipped, herbivorous dinosaurs, and she is a leading expert on the stegosaurs. Susannah has published over fifty papers in peer-reviewed literature, and regularly appears on radio and TV talking about dinosaurs. She has previously won the Geological Society of London's Lyell Fund and the Palaeontological Association's Hodson Award, both for notable contributions by an early career researcher. In 2019 she featured as a National Geographic woman of impact.

Dave Hone

Dave Hone is a palaeontologist and writer. His research focuses on the behaviour and ecology of the dinosaurs and their flying relatives, the pterosaurs. He writes extensively online about palaeontology and science outreach and regularly contributes to other media outlets as well as acting as a scientific consultant. His first book, the The Tyrannosaur Chronicles, *is out now with Bloomsbury.*

Clarissa Koos

Clarissa Koos lives in Bozeman, Montana, and is currently studying to become a scientific illustrator at Montana State University and plans to graduate in 2023. She is in the Directed Interdisciplinary Studies (D.I.S.) program through the honors college studying palaeontology, biology and art. Clarissa is creating illustrations for the Museum of the Rockies, as well as for graduate students and professors. She has been going to dinosaur dig sites since she was 11 years old. Clarissa has volunteered at the Dino Day events at the Burke Museum where she has shared her scientific passions with visitors.

GLOSSARY

ARCHOSAURS

Group of reptiles that includes the ancestors of all dinos.

BADLANDS

Perfect dino-hunting territory. This a type of terrain that's experienced A LOT of erosion, so old rock (which might contain dino fossils) is near the surface.

CAMBRIAN EXPLOSION

Period of MASSIVE evolutionary change; started about 540 million years ago.

CAT SCANS

Scans that use super powerful X-rays to let scientists look inside fossils without breaking them.

CHICXULUB

Mexican port town. The asteroid that scientists think wiped out the dinos smashed into shallow water near here.

COPROLITE

Fossilized poo.

CRETACEOUS PERIOD

The Cretaceous Period started 145.5 million years ago; Earth is now home to all kinds of dinosaur groups!

FOSSIL

Any preserved remains of something that was once alive.

JURASSIC COAST

A stretch of shoreline in south-west England. World-famous for incredible Jurassic-Period dino finds.

JURASSIC PERIOD

The Jurassic Period started 199.6 million years ago. Golden Age of the dinos.

MESOZOIC ERA

Made up of the Triassic, Jurassic and Cretaceous Periods.

PALAEONTOLOGIST

Best job ever. (Someone who studies fossils to learn about the history of life on Earth.)

PANGAEA

The giant supercontinent on which dinos first evolved.

PERMIAN EXTINCTION

This mass-extinction wiped out 90% of life on Earth. Thankfully, dino ancestors survived it!

PTEROSAURS

The first backboned creatures to fly through the skies.

ORNITHISCIANS

The 'bird-hipped' family of dinos.

SAURISCHIANS

The 'lizard-hipped' family of dinos.

TETRAPOD

Four-limbed animals; includes dinos and some birds, and mammals.

THEROPODS

A family of dinos that stood on two legs; includes T. rex and Velociraptor; ancestors of today's birds.

TRIASSIC PERIOD

The Triassic Period started 252.2 million years ago; Welcome, first dinosaurs!

ABOUT THE AUTHOR

Dougie Poynter is a musician, songwriter, designer and author. He has been obsessed with natural history and dinosaurs from the age of three when he visited the Natural History Museum with his mum. He is passionate about the natural world and is a keen conservationist, working with charities such as WWF, Greenpeace and 5 Gyres. He is committed to cleaning up the planet and was instrumental in the campaign to ban microplastics in the UK.

Dougie has been the bass player of the band McFly since 2003 and, along with bandmate Tom Fletcher, is behind the bestselling picture book series 'The Dinosaur That Pooped' illustrated by Garry Parsons, the series has sold more than 1 million copies. Dougie was also a member of the super-group McBusted and in 2011 was the winner of the jungle set show I'm a Celebrity Get Me Out of Here.

ACKNOWLEDGEMENTS

The wonderful team at Macmillan Children's Books – special thanks to Gaby Morgan, Emma Young, Emma S. Young, Amy Boxshall, Janene Spencer, Rachel Vale, Laura Carter, Kat McKenna, Sarah Clarke, Jo Hardacre and Sarah Plows.

To my agents Stephanie Thwaites and Isobel Gahan at Curtis Brown. My manager Alex Weston at Riverman Management.

My family: Mum, Jazz and Paul.

To all the incredible contributors to this book. My heartfelt thanks to Susannah Maidment, Sarah Slaughter, Clarissa Koos, Dave Hone and Steve Brusatte. My band McFly – Harry, Danny and Tom for being the beating heart of everything and for being my family. And to anyone else who has supported me in anyway, I appreciate it in more ways than I can put down in words.